La Pizza

Nikko Amandonico's

La Pizza
The True Story from Naples

Photographs Ewa-Marie Rundquist

Recipe photographs Giuseppe Bigliardi

Text Natalia Borri

Essays Ian Thomson

MITCHELL BEAZLEY

FIRST PUBLISHED IN GREAT BRITAIN IN 2001 BY MITCHELL BEAZLEY,
AN IMPRINT OF OCTOPUS PUBLISHING GROUP LTD, 2-4 HERON QUAYS, LONDON E 14 4JP
THIS IS A NIKKOBOOK PUBLICATION

A CIP RECORD FOR THIS BOOK IS AVAILABLE FROM THE BRITISH LIBRARY

EDITOR: ÅSE INDE/NIKKOBOOK IN CO-OPERATION WITH EVA-MARIA WESTBERG/PRISMA
LITHOGRAPHY: PRISMAGRAF, VERONA, ITALY
PRINTING AND BINDING: GRAPHICOM, VICENZA, ITALY 2001

ISBN: 1 84000 452 5

Contents

Although I grew up in Sweden in the Fifties, my earliest memories of food are strongly associated with southern Italy. The meatballs at our home smelt of nutmeg, tomatoes and parsley, and were definitely not eaten with sweet cowberry jam. As in all Italian families, our home life revolved around mother's kitchen domains. There we had meal times that were almost holy when the food parcels from mother's and father's relations in Taranto arrived: *olio d'oliva, salsiccia piccante* and *origano*. In truth, I believe that the Italian food is the reason why I moved back to Italy in my adult years.

This is my first cookbook and it's about the most appreciated and perhaps mistreated dish from the southern Italian kitchen – the pizza. In a book about the pizza, it is impossible not to describe its creative inventor, the Neapolitan, and Naples, Italy's liveliest town. I have eaten pizza in every corner of the world, but it tastes better than anywhere else in Naples, its home town. This book is a tribute to the town, the people and the Neapolitan spirit. But above all, it is a tribute to the world's most widely distributed food – La Pizza.

The book contains the classic Neapolitan pizza recipes – Marinara and Margherita. I have created the rest of the recipes in the book with ingredients and flavours from the southern Italian kitchen. The recipes are created for all those of us who like to bake pizzas at home in our own kitchens. Use them as they are or as an inspiration for new varieties. I am quite sure that the *Associazione Vera Pizza Napoletana* would utterly condemn my creations, but as a good southern Italian, I know that rules are there to… not perhaps break, but to bend them somewhat has never harmed.

Nikko

Naples and pizza

by Ian Thomson

'The spirit of Naples, ragamuffin capital of the Italian south, lives on the street. There is a *dolce far niente* – a sweet chaos of bustling markets, dark-eyed beauties, artful dodgers and Neapolitan widows swaddled in black. Wares are laid out on the pavement. You can choose anything from Barbie dolls to watermelons. The city is a hive of beetling activity.

One-time Arcady of Bourbon kings and queens, Naples is also grandiose baroque. Amid the age-old poverty there are castles, churches and palaces languishing in decayed majesty. 'See Naples and die,' they used to say. It is still the most beautiful of Italian cities. To look out across the Bay of Naples is a visual education in the grand style. The sea is a wonderful Pernod-green, and further out, a darkly, deeply beautiful blue. In summer there is a liquid softness to the air; a perfume of dead flowers, sea wrack, wood fires.

The city's dusty splendour owes something to the souks of the Middle East, something to the Levant. You can't hurry in Naples. There is an atmosphere of intoxicated self-forgetfulness and a healthy Oriental contempt for time. If the Milanese take showers (for time-saving efficiency), the Neapolitans prefer a long, hot bath.

The pizza, culinary pride of Naples, is a poor man's dish. And Naples is a poor city. Some of its tumbledown dwellings are so cramped, they barely let the daylight in. 'Where the sun does not enter,' runs a Neapolitan proverb, 'the doctor does.' The one-room hovels of Naples, called *bassi*, often double up as sweatshops. Down in the Victorian half-light children are seen hammering at a piece of shoe-leather, or stitching some counterfeit *couture* dress.

Naples, poor in resources, is nevertheless rich in creativity. The pizza was born amid the city's carnival exuberance of life. Nothing, absolutely nothing that can be managed by the human digestive system is wasted in Naples. During the hungry years of the Second World War, the city's seaside aquarium was ransacked by famished locals who boiled the tropical fish for a variety of unusual pizza and pasta dishes. Neapolitans give this resourcefulness a name – *l'arte di arrangiarsi*, the art of getting by. They are masters of imaginative improvisation and have a sardonic, devil-may-care humour. A homeless Neapolitan living rough on the streets carried a placard: 'Reduced to these circumstances by my brother-in-law'. Some Neapolitans reputedly have arranged to be run over so that they can claim insurance.

There are over 500 pizzerias in this helter-skelter city. Neapolitan taxi-drivers talk about pizza the way London cabbies talk about the weather. Careering over pavements, hurtling the wrong way up one-way streets, your driver will patiently explain that every ancient civilization under the sun had its own version of the pizza, from the ancient Egyptians to the Romans of Pompeii. But the first pizza was invented in Naples. It was the Neapolitans who originally combined succulent red tomatoes (*pummarola*, in their dialect) with a flour-and-water dough, leading to a worldwide gastronomic revolution. The earliest textual recipe for the pizza appeared in Naples in 1858, but the dish had been known to the Neapolitans at least since the 18th century.

Today the pizza is the most successful mass-culture food in the world and it has even reached a

'We invented the pizza, and what do the Americans give us in return? A box to carry it in!'

"Noi Napoletani ammë ˈnventatë ˈa pizza ...

... e gli Ammericani in cambio cosa c'hanno dato?

"'O scatolë per trasportarla!"

far-flung country like Haiti, land of voodoo. In the Haitian capital of Port-au-Prince there is a bar called the Café Napoli. Faded Kodachrome photographs of Mount Vesuvius (and Sophia Loren) adorn the walls, and the Neapolitan owner, Signora Aïda Esposito, offers excellent pizza. However, it's not quite the real McCoy. Sacrilegiously (for a Neapolitan), Aïda toasts her pizzas in an electric oven. Back in Naples, Aïda's home town, only wood fires would be allowed.

Sadly, many think that the pizza was born in America. As one Neapolitan protested: 'We invented the pizza, and what do the Americans give us in return? A box to carry it in!' Eisenhower, the US President, told the press in 1952 that he had eaten better pizza in New York than in Naples; it caused a diplomatic uproar.

There is just one authentic pizza. This is the tomato version in its two original varieties. Namely, the Marinara, with garlic, oregano and olive oil; and the Margherita, with mozzarella and basil. Everything else is dross, especially those doughy monstrosities with egg, pineapple or Würstel toppings which tourists like to eat. Fortunately the *Associazione Vera Pizza Napoletana* sets out to defend the original from imitations.

Yet the Neapolitan distaste for other people's pizzas – the fake variety – is curious in a city which has made a fortune out of manufacturing fakes. If, as they say, Naples is halfway to Baghdad, then the city's Casbah is the bustling Camorra market known as the Forcella. The *contrabbandisti* here will try and sell you counterfeit bottles of Fernet Branca liqueur, phials of ersatz Chanel No. 5 ('But our perfume's much better than the real French stuff – a single drop, madam, and you'll be well appreciated'), fake brands of whisky and – typically – artificial Louis Vuitton handbags ('Those costing 500,000 lire, we'll give to you for just 15,000!'). But there is one thing these wily old tricksters will never, ever sell you, and that's a fake pizza.

It's fitting that the original Naples speciality should be a tomato-based pizza, since red is the city's spiritual colour. Thousands of Neapolitans ward off the evil eye with a bright red amulet shaped like a twisted pepper. They hang these gee-gaws over their pizzerias, from taxi mirrors and on chains around their necks. Naples is the superstitious capital of Europe and blood especially is endowed with magical properties. Countless religious shrines have been built on sites where the hallowed stuff has spilled. Blood is balm for the Neapolitans and to dream of its liquid ruby red is considered extremely lucky. Much hoo-ha is made in Naples about the bi-annual liquefaction of the blood of San Gennaro, the city's patron. The saint's blood is held in two glass ampoules in a special chapel. It's pure voodoo: if the holy grume fails to melt, disaster will ensue. 'Naples 2, Milan 3: San Gennaro Still No Miracle', ran a famous newspaper headline after Naples lost a football match.

The tomato-red of the pizza, like the blood of San Gennaro, is symbolic of all that's good in Naples. It's an antidote to the bad Camorra blood that stains the city's dark streets. The miracle (so-called) of San Gennaro should not be missed. Under the rococo dome of the cathedral a brass band plays the Italian national anthem, while Neapolitan notables (stiffly starched in white tails and ties) mingle with nuns of every order.

Overdressed *carabinieri* resemble extras from a Fellini movie, their helmets plumed with nodding feathers. Forty yellow taxis are parked one behind the other in the aisles. Strapped to the rack of each roof is a giant silver bust of each of the 40 saints that Neapolitans associate with San Gennaro.

After the blood has liquefied, the taxis reverse out of the Duomo and drive with due solemnity (this is difficult, given the chaos of Neapolitan traffic) to the nearby convent of Santa Chiara where the archbishop administers a *Te Deum*. Time was when each bust was placed on a monstrance and shouldered in procession by young men, huffing and puffing under the weight of the holy silver. But even ramshackle Naples has kept apace with the modern age – taxis are quicker.

Victorian travellers to Naples dismissed the San Gennaro ritual as pre-Christian or 'heathen', and they were not far wrong. In one of his perverse, hallucinated newspaper articles, Pier Paolo Pasolini spoke of the Neapolitans as a people who had rejected the modern world. He described them as a desert tribe, camped in their piazzas, waiting for the end, choosing death over life.

Naples always has been a death-haunted city. In the devastated postwar years, pizzas were often sold on credit; if the customer were to die unexpectedly before payment was due (seven days later), his would have been a free pizza. Thus even the world's most joyous food – the Neapolitan pizza – was touched by graveyard comedy. Only in Naples are baroque funeral hearses still pulled through the streets lugubriously by 12 black horses. The very wealthy (Camorra bosses, millionaire pizza magnates) can afford such a kitchy send-off. The hearses belong to the Naples undertaker Bellomunno and Co, optimistically named after the Neapolitan dialect for *bello mondo* – beautiful world. Yet there is nothing very beautiful about these wedding-cake hearses; they recall the tawdry grandiloquence of the Spanish Bourbons, who misruled Naples for 126 years until 1860.

It was during Bourbon rule that Naples first flourished as a tourist attraction. A museum was

opened to house the treasures recently unearthed at Pompeii, while English gentlemen flocked to the city as part of the Grand Tour. Naples then became the third largest city in Europe after Vienna and Paris. In 1793 a Frenchman found it 'the only place in Italy which really feels like a capital… a Court which is a proper court and a glittering one… the same busy and lively atmosphere that one finds in Paris or London and which does not even exist in Rome'.

In superstitious Naples, even gambling is a matter of religion. Alexandre Dumas *père* relates how he overheard a Neapolitan wretch praying that 'God would ask San Gennaro to grant him a win on the lottery'. To dream of this saint was tantamount to dreaming of the Naples football star Diego Maradona – you couldn't get more lucky. Keen to find out more about dreams and numbers in Naples, I contacted Don Pasquale. For 40 years this hunchbacked octogenarian has sold lottery tickets at the Via Roma entrance to the Galleria Umberto, that fabulous cross between a railway station and a church.

Togged out in pork-pie and braces, munching toothlessly on a hot Margherita, Don Pasquale put me in the mystical picture. 'Wake up in the morning with an image of a naked woman in your head – place a bet on number 21; of blood, 18; of the soul in purgatory, 85; of Diego Maradona, 23. So try your luck on those.'

The weekly state lottery in the heart of old Naples was packed with gamblers shouting and jostling fever-ishly. A master of ceremonies tried uselessly to silence the crowd as a blind-folded boy pulled out the lucky numbers from a revolving cage. Curiously, when the number 34 was extracted, uproarious applause went up, along with much shaking of hands and embracing. Corresponding to the dream of a stubborn or difficult person, 34 is regarded by Neapolitans with religious dread; when extracted, it is cause for celebration.

Naples today is a hectic confusion of decayed majesty, pickpocketing crime and downright *miseria* or poverty. Nothing much has changed since the foppish Casanova, visiting the city 250 years ago, was robbed of 20 silk handkerchiefs in the space of a month. The traffic-congested streets of the historical centre are foul with exhaust fumes. Even before cars were common in Naples, Mark Twain marvelled at the city: 'Why a

Busy at all times of day, the Di Matteo pizzeria, in the heart of the old town, is famous for its excellent deep-fried pizza – delicious with a ricotta and ham filling. Or, if you feel like a quick snack, you can get to the counter directly from the street and order a pizza a libretto, *with its double fold and ready to eat with your hands, just like in the old days.*

  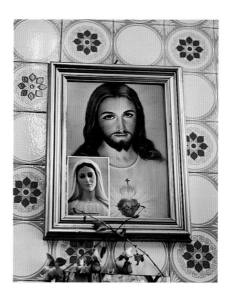

thousand people are not run over every day is a mystery no man can solve.'

One's first impression of Naples is likely to be of sleaze on a grand scale, if not of a drastic filth. The snobbish English art critic John Ruskin dismissed Naples, unfairly, as 'certainly the most disgusting place in Europe'. True, the ill-famed Spanish Quarter now has a population density comparable only to that of Hong Kong. Stone memorials there record thousands of cholera victims (unbelievably, the last epidemic broke out in Naples as recently as 1973). Yet with its balconies dripping with white linen and its streets festooned with pizza-shop flags, the Spanish Quarter has its own picturesqueness. People sing there: '*Si nun si canta se more*' — 'If you don't sing you're dead', an absolutely vintage Neapolitan expression. Northern Europeans unaccustomed to spontaneaous song are either charmed or embarrassed by these outbursts.

Ineluctably, Naples begins to weave its own special magic on the visitor. Down by the water's edge the *venditore di volante* (literally 'sellers of flying things') amble past with clusters of bobbing balloons and multi-coloured kites for children. Ice-cream and coconut vendors drowse beneath sun parasols striped with the blue and white of the Naples football team. Further out to sea lies one of the most extraordinary sights in the world – 'a little bit of heaven fallen upon earth', the Neapolitans call it. Slumbering tantalizingly on the horizon like semi-submerged leviathans are Capri, Ischia and Procida. Slow boats chug steadily towards the three famous islands, dots of white in the numinous ether. And way to the left, destructive Vesuvius is dimly visible in the haze.

Allied forces were spellbound by that same magical panorama in 1944. Many of the American soldiers who stumbled down the crowded gangplanks into Naples' brilliant sunlight were of Italian extraction. And in the emotional heart of wartime Naples they got drunk, trafficked in contraband cigarettes (cartons of 'Luckies', of course), nylon stockings and penicillin. They experienced such un-American phenomena as red wine, pasta with clams and... the pizza. Indeed, many US troops in Naples ate pizza for the first time and impatiently lined up for another seafront Margherita or Marinara. You could say that fast-food was born right there in 1940s Naples with the Allied occupation. Hot, savoury, tasty, nutritious, pizzas were speedily devoured by GIs and marines who took the recipes back home with them to the US. In New York the first pizzeria had opened in 1895. But after the war whole chains of pizzerias mushroomed overnight in Manhattan, Brooklyn and the Bronx.

Indeed, it was in New York that the pizza truly became the Pizza. Italo-Americans were proud of their takeaway outlets and spoke of a *pizza shoppa*, a *pizza joba* or *pizza storo* (they said 'Shurrup!' quite a lot, too). Inevitably the *Americani* are a dying breed today; fourth- or fifth-generation Italo-Americans are forgetting the land of their ancestors. Many of them scandalously believe that the pizza is an American, not a Neapolitan, invention. ('How do you say "pizza" in Italian?' they might ask sacrilegiously). Yet Naples would not exist without the pizza, nor the pizza without Naples. As our taxi-driver says: '*Com'è bella Napoli!*' Then he flashes a gold tooth and asks you about his uncle's pizzeria. Do you know it?

THAT'S AMORE

(That's Love)

Words by
JACK BROOKS

Music by
HARRY WARREN

Myth and history of the Neapolitan pizza

by Ian Thomson

The origins of the pizza are lost in the mists of antiquity. A variety of the doughy disc existed at the time of Jesus Christ. So say the Neapolitans. At Christmas in Naples every family brings out a model crib with a terracotta pizza-maker among the Bethlehem shepherds. Today there is no *pizza alla Betlemme* in Naples, but there ought to be. Christianity has left only a translucent veneer – a snail's trail – over the superstitious surface of Neapolitan Catholicism. Every street corner shows an illuminated altar to the Madonna, but these Neapolitan Virgins are less Christian than paganized sea-queens. Garnished with fluorescent neon hoops, they are reincarnations of Greek and Roman divinities.

The classical poet Hesiod relates that Demeter, the ancient Greek goddess of corn, was lavished with an offering of 'flat bread made of water, flour and mint'. Cooked to a crisp over a wood-fire, this minty confection was the pizza's distant ancestor. The modern Neapolitan speciality harks back to the dawn of civilization and pre-dates our use of wooden or ceramic tableware. As a substitute plate, primitive man used an edible disc of baked dough.

Later, when classical Greek myth was absorbed into Roman culture, Demeter was transformed into the Latin corn goddess Ceres. A temple was dedicated to her in Rome in 496 BC after a terrible famine. The grateful populace brought Ceres votive offerings of baked corn in the shape of platters.

Pizza myths have passed like a runner's baton from generation to generation changed and embellished, but they always come back to Naples. Mount Vesuvius especially is rich in pizza lore. One day the Olympian blacksmith Vulcan closed his fiery furnace in the core of the volcano and set off for lunch. However, his wife Venus had failed to rustle up any food and, fearing Vulcan's wrath, hastily improvised a dish. What she made was a *focaccia* flat cake, cooked lovingly on the volcano's glowing larval embers. Venus then dipped the toast in goat's milk and garnished it with berries and fragrant herbs. In a couple of minutes, lunch was ready. Vulcan liked it so much that he ordered Venus to make him the same delicious hot meal daily. Then the contented blacksmith asked his wife to reveal the recipe to the townspeople of Vesuvius so they too could savour the gastronomic delight of this prototype pizza. Legend adds that Venus planted an essential ingredient of our modern pizza – tomatoes – on the volcano's side. Indeed, today the egg-shaped San Marzano (the best tomatoes, say the Neapolitans, in the world) grow plump and juicy on the Vesuvius foothills.

Vesuvius – Goethe's 'peak of hell rising out of paradise' – erupted on 24 August AD 79. Strange fiery symbols shot across the bay of Naples as Vulcan's mythical furnace swallowed Pompeii in pumice-dust and ash. Today at Pompeii you can eat a tourist's pizza served in wedge-shaped portions. But in the petrified ancient city there is evidence that the *gens pompeiana* themselves ate a sort of pizza. Excavations have revealed bas-reliefs at Pompeii depicting spacious hearths which recall modern-day pizzeria ovens. Carbonized foodstuffs dug up from the city's lava-swamped houses – olives, anchovy fragments, onions – show that all the ingredients for a pizza existed in Roman times.

It is easy to imagine the imperial Ceasars dining on thin, baked dough garnished with buffalo milk cheese, marjoram and *pummarola* sauce.

Today at the Naples Archaeologial Museum you can see circular Pompeii cakes resembling burnt tarts. Alexandre Dumas *pére*, who was briefly chief custodian of the museum, reckoned they were early pizzas. In his delightful memoir of Naples, *Il Corricolo*, the Frenchman claimed the pizza was a winter dish for the Neapolitan poor. He wrote of their poverty: 'While the gentleman feeds his dogs with white bread, the people live on roots and herbs, eked out with an insufficient quantity of coarse bread.' This coarse bread was the basis for crude 19th-century pizza.

It is hard to believe, with its twin camel-shaped mounds smoking gently in the distance, that Vesuvius could have engulfed an entire city in its lava. Yet the English poet Shelley was made so terrified by his ascent of the volcano in 1818 that, over-come by nausea before he reached the summit, he was revived by a slice of pizza and a dose of opium in a nearby church. This church, the Hermitage of San Salvador, is today deconsecrated and overgrown with nettles. But a pizzeria next door, called I Love Vesuvius, does a roaring tourist trade.

Tracing the origins of this timeless food is problematic. Allegedly the Ancient Egyptians were the first to discover a leavening agent for bread, but there are numerous conflicting theories of the pizza's true birth. In 1991, for example, the Chinese Historical Society pitched a strong claim for a 13th-century flat bread made from sweet rice flour and spices called *ping tse*. Today in Turkey you can eat a meat pizza – a *lahmacun* – which was an Ottoman invention. Nevertheless, modern scholars mostly agree that the pizza is an Italo-Mediterranean con-coction and has been known in Italy for at least 3,000 years. Charmingly, the Esperanto for pizza is *itala pasteio* – Italian pie.

One thing is certain, the Neapolitans were the first to combine juicy red tomatoes with a flour and water base. This occurred in the late 17th century when the tomato was still regarded with some sus-picion since its importation 200 years earlier from Peru. No cutlery was provided with these earliest Neapolitan pizzas and even today the sizzling doughy bread is best eaten with fingers. Could this be why the pizza is such a refined dish? Ovid, in his *Art of Love*, implied that an absence of cutlery was eminently civilized. In the classical world we ate only with our hands. There were no forks used at the Homeric beach barbecues; in scorning knives and forks, the pizza is a prince among dishes.

In the contemporary mythology of Naples the pizza has become a foreigner's cliché of the city, along with spaghetti, Vesuvius, Enrico Caruso, mandolins, street musicians, Sophia Loren and the Neapolitans' riotous sense of theatre. Traditionally, Neapolitans are indeed flammable and they are masters at the art of gesture. A marvellous 18th-century guide called *La Mimica Degli Antichi Investigata nel Gestire Napoletana* (The Mimicry of the Ancient People Interpreted Through the Gestures of the Neapolitans) lists ten possible gestures for expressing rage. These range from 'biting one's hands' to 'pretending to bite one's elbows'. All these and other animations can be seen today in Neapolitan pizzerias where dough is endlessly and expertly kneaded, spread and beaten just as it was in Pompeii 80 years after the birth of Christ.

Ultimately, the pizza is a simple, poor man's dish. But the stranger coming to Naples for the first time should avoid judging over-hastily and dismissing the dish as 'gastronomically challenged'. The best Neapolitan pizzas can make anything outside Italy look and taste like an old tobacco pouch. Naturally there are expectations. In 1883 the grumpy English traveller August Hare was offered a dish in Naples which he described as the 'horrible condiment called pizza made of dough baked with garlic, rancid bacon and strong cheese'. My guess is that Hare was unlucky; he was fobbed off with a piece of unappetizing dough. The genuine Neapolitan pizza is a glory fit for the gods.

napoleta

Pizzerias and pizza-makers in Naples

A professional pizza-maker turns out at least 60 pizzas an hour.

In Naples, you can eat a pizza in the oldest pizzeria in the whole world, pizzeria Port'Alba, at 18, Via Port'Alba, since 1830. And where else but in Naples could the first pizzerias have come into existence? Neapolitan pizza-makers are justifiably proud of this record, as they are of the fact that the advent of the first Neapolitan pizzerias represents the arrival of the first take-away restaurants and fast-food joints in history.

Originally, pizzerias were simple workshops where pizzas were prepared and cooked, but not served. Here, the first pizza-makers distributed their pizzas through travelling salesmen who went around town selling them. Instead of the cardboard boxes universally used today to transport pizzas, they had metal containers, called *stufe* or 'ovens', which were round, had holes to keep the flavour intact and internal shelves, each of which housed one pizza. The salesmen wandered through Naples with the *stufa* on their heads. They wrapped a cloth into a doughnut shape (called a *curuoglio*) upon which the container would sit, to give it better balance, and they carried a foldable table (called *lanzuno*), onto which they would set the container in order to take out a pizza whenever they made a sale.

The citizens of Naples could count on a scrumptious street pizza at every hour of the day and they would eat it then and there, while it was still steaming hot and runny, and strictly with their hands. The only handicap was that these metal containers didn't maintain the heat for very long, so the last pizzas, which were inevitably cold, were sold more cheaply.

In the meantime, the workshops also began selling their pizzas directly; their customers would eat their pizzas on the street, standing or sitting on steps in the road outside the pizzeria. A business like this didn't have heavy costs. All you needed was a room, an oven, a marble work surface to knead the dough and a shelf for the flour. You didn't even have to provide your customers with a plate, since pizzas were folded over and eaten with hands. No beverages were served, either. If customers were thirsty, they could purchase a glass of cool water from one of the many *aquaioli* in circulation on the streets of Naples. So, the first pizzerias were authentic take-aways, and as today's Neapolitan pizza-makers are wont to say, with a hint of amicable sarcasm: 'When we invented take-away, the Americans were still playing cowboys and Indians!'

The more successful workshops had more than one salesman travelling around with their pizzas. When the *stufa* was empty, the salesman would leave it on a bench near the entrance and pick up a new one full of pizzas ready to be sold. Perhaps more and more customers would sit down on the same bench, thus originating the process that would gradually transform those antique workshops into modern-day pizzerias. Some pizza-makers made good profits and were able to expand their premises. So, in the early 19th century, some pizzerias put out benches along their walls where people would stop off to eat a pizza and have a chat. Then came the first tables, the first chairs and the first knives and forks. Sometimes the tables were walled into the building on one side. This happened because pizza-makers often ran up debts to enlarge their pizzerias and take in more and more customers. The walled tables became part of the structure of the building and as such couldn't be confiscated if business was bad and debts couldn't be met. At the pizzeria Da Michele, fortunately things went so well that today it is still one of the best known pizzerias in town, with its simple decor, white tiled walls, wooden chairs and marble tables, now, at last, no longer walled in.

In these prototype fast-food restaurants, Neapolitan pizza-makers perfected their own inimitable means of expression, by gesticulating, calling and shouting – an authentic technique for attracting customers. The Neapolitan writer Francesco Mastriani, in his novel *Ciccio, il pizzaiuolo di Borgo Loreto* set in Naples in 1836, narrates: 'The pizza-maker is busy beating and spreading the dough, making that noise that is so particular to pizza-makers, that they make as loud as possible to show that their pizzeria is full from morning to evening and that the dough doesn't lie idle on the counter for an instant.'

Still today, when pizza-makers are in the right mood, you can hear colourful, time-honoured expressions wafting through the pizzeria together with the fragrance of the pizzas. *'Jammo cu' 'a pala!'* ('Move it with the shovel') – the pizza-maker who has just finished topping the pizza invites a colleague to come over with the baker's shovel to put it in the oven; *'Ma che so', briosce?'* ('What are they, brioches?') – an exclamation in praise of the dough, whose friability is so perfect as to seem a brioche. Today there are more than 500 pizzerias in Naples. The profession of the pizza-maker is so deeply entrenched in the culture, history and tradition of Naples that, every year at Christmas, in the typical model representations of the Nativity in the shop windows on the Spaccanapoli, the picturesque avenue running right through the town centre, there is always a pizzeria among the inns of Bethlehem and a pizza-maker among the shepherds.

Pizza Marinara

Pizzeria Da Michele is one of the oldest and most original pizzerias in Naples. Founded in 1847 by Salvatore Condurro, in Via Cesare Sersale, today it is run by Michele, Salvatore's grandson, and Antonio, Michele's son – at least three generations of pizza-makers devoted to keeping the tradition and history of the authentic Neapolitan pizza alive. Signor Michele and Signor Antonio are, like all self-respecting citizens of Naples, deeply proud of the success that pizza enjoys all over the world, and yet, when you mention the names of the many varieties of pizza available in every corner of the Earth, including Italy and even Naples itself, they can't help turning up their noses. Because, for Signor Michele and Signor Antonio, there is only one pizza worthy of the name. And that is the type made with tomato in its two original versions: Marinara, with garlic, oregano and oil; and Margherita, with mozzarella and basil. Everything else just isn't pizza. Not real Neapolitan pizza, anyway. In strict compliance with this credo, Pizzeria Da Michele has been serving nothing but pizza Margherita and pizza Marinara since 1847. Outside Naples, pizza Marinara is often called pizza Napoletana, as if to emphasize its authenticity. But,

even though there isn't a single anchovy or prawn in sight, Marinara is its real name. This isn't a paradoxical joke that Neapolitans play on unsuspecting tourists. The reason is that the name doesn't refer to seafood but to the times when fishermen, after a night at sea, would stop off at the bakery and, extremely hungry but in a hurry to get home, would ask for a pizza that was light and quick. In fact, pizza Marinara is about as basic and frugal as pizzas go, which still today makes it the perfect snack. Real pizza connoisseurs, however, like to take their time and slowly savour its delicious simplicity, as the taste of fresh tomato and oregano mingles with garlic and extra-virgin olive oil in an exquisite balance of flavours, set off by the unmistakable aroma of the wood-fuelled oven it is cooked in.

Raffaele Esposito evidently wasn't of the same opinion, when, in 1889, he went to court to cook a pizza for Queen Margherita of Italy. When making up his mind what kind of pizza to make, he didn't opt for the classic and simple pizza Marinara, partly because he thought it inappropriate to serve the queen a pizza topped with garlic, and partly because he wanted to display his talent with slightly more elaborate recipes.

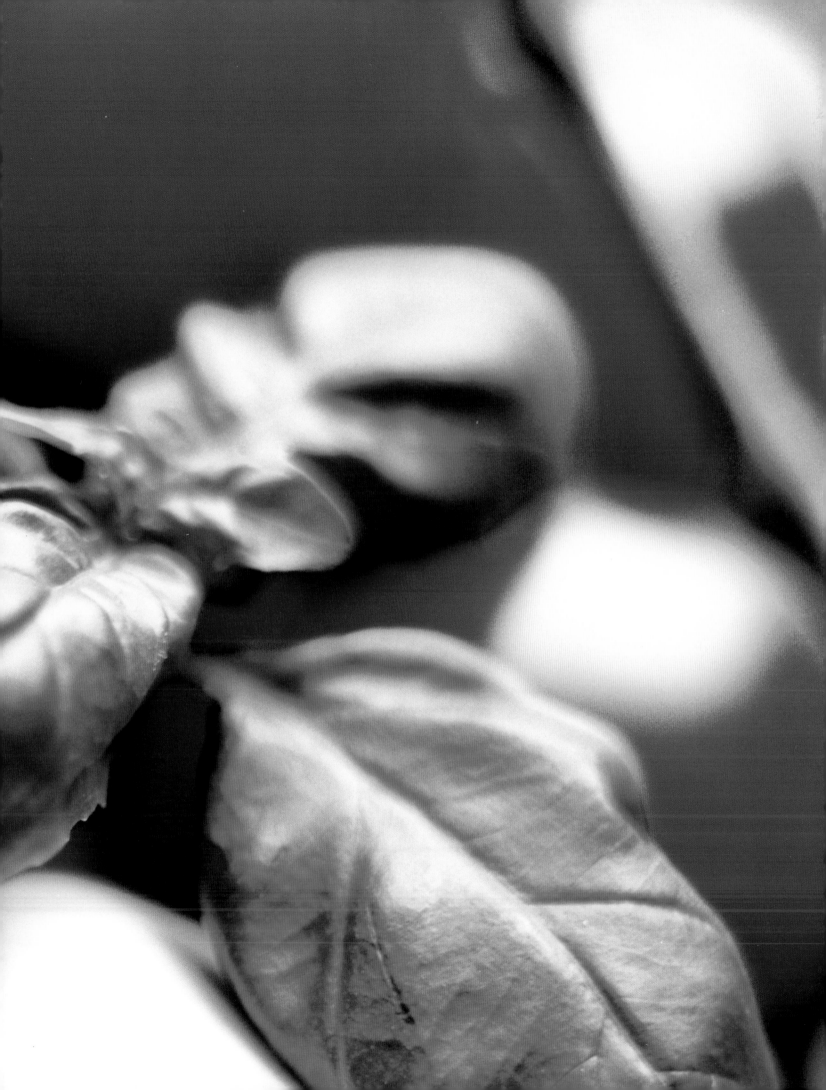

Brandi

Pizza Margherita

'This is where pizza Margherita was born, 100 years ago.' We are in the heart of old Naples, a few yards from Piazza del Plebiscito, on Salita Sant'Anna di Palazzo, at the start of the thronging Via Chiaia. The marble sign dominates the entrance to Naples' most famous pizzeria – Pizzeria Brandi. This is where, on the 11th June 1889, pizza Margherita was born. And this is where today's owner Vincenzo Pagnani wants, with this placard, to commemorate the centenary of the world's most famous pizza, the Margherita – the very queen of pizzas.

The story of both pizza Margherita and the Pizzeria Brandi blends in with the history of the Naples of the time, which, after centuries of Spanish dominion, thanks to the legendary feats of the Thousand, led by Giuseppe Garibaldi, became part of the Kingdom of Italy, founded in 1861 with the proclamation of Vittorio Emmanuele II as King of Italy. In 1889 the Pizzeria Brandi had another name. It was rather oddly called *Pietro... e basta così*, which means 'Peter.... and what more could you want?'. The king of Italy was Umberto I, the son of Vittorio Emmanuele II. Nothing could have been further from the rulers of the House of Savoy than a pizzeria in Naples. Not only because the king lived hundreds of miles further north in Turin, and went down to Naples only for the occasional brief sojourn in the Napoleonic palace of Capodimonte. But also because, up until that time, pizza was strictly for the poor and pizzerias were noisy, uncouth places where the lower classes went. That is until that famous day in June 1889. King Umberto I and his wife, Queen Margherita of Savoy, were in residence at Capodimonte. Weary of the over-elaborate French-style recipes that the court chef regularly cooked for

the queen, she expressed a wish to taste a local speciality about which she had probably heard some lady-in-waiting or domestic staff raving. So she ordered the *Ufficio di Bocca* (a kind of royal tastebud department) to summon to Capodimonte the pizza-maker who was presumably considered to make the best pizzas around – Raffaele Esposito, of the pizzeria *Pietro... e basta così*. Don Raffaele could hardly decline such an invitation and so, accompanied by his wife Pasqualina Brandi (of the same family after whom the pizzeria is named today), he went to court, bringing with him some simple ingredients and the few tools he needed. In the royal oven, Don Raffaele made three types of pizza: one with *cecinielli* (small fish like whitebait), one with olive oil and cheese and one with tomato, mozzarella and basil. In the evening of the very same day, Raffaele received a letter delivered by hand by the head of the *Servizi da Tavola della Real Casa* (the Royal Household Culinary Service) in person. This letter is on display in the pizzeria today and it affirms that the pizzas made for the queen 'were found to be very good'.

This was by no means the only gratification for Don Raffaele; his pizzeria was given the official title of *Fornitore della Real Casa*, or Purveyor to the Royal House, and from that day on, the bourgeoisie, which had always snubbed pizzas and pizzerias, changed its mind about this humble food of the poor.

As one might suppose, these events made quite a stir in Naples, and so it was that the facts were, with the passage of time, embellished and enriched with every manner of imaginative detail. In this spirit, one hears of the rendezvous at Capodimonte between Raffaele Esposito and the queen, on which occasion, when asked what the pizza with tomato, mozzarella and basil that so pleased the sovereign was called, Don Raffaele is said to have replied, 'Margherita, in your honour, your Majesty.' And one also hears that it was a spontaneous stroke of genius that inspired Don Raffaele to create a pizza with which to glorify the queen of Italy by uniting the three colours – green, white and red – of the Italian flag. If the truth be known, earlier documents prove that this kind of pizza already existed in the Neapolitan gastronomical tradition. In 1866, a Neapolitan author called Emmanuele Rocco wrote a piece dedicated *al pizzajuolo*, to the pizza-maker, in which he mentions 'pizza with finely sliced mozzarella, tomato and basil leaves'. Be that as it may. For even if Don Raffaele invented nothing new and fobbed the queen off with a pizza made to a recipe devoid of any originality, he must have made it well and so, if the sovereign liked it, it is thanks to his extraordinary culinary talent. From that famous 11th June, pizza with tomato, mozzarella and basil became known to all as the queen of pizzas – pizza Margherita.

Vincenzo Pagnani is the owner of the ancient Pizzeria Brandi. This was the place where, in 1889, the pizza Margherita got its name, after Queen Margherita of Italy. But the queen probably didn't imagine that, over 100 years later, she would become the testimonial in an advertising campaign or that she would star in posters and fliers all over Naples. Signor Pagnani is astute, and he is well aware of the fact that not everyone has had a queen to dinner. It's a powerful weapon and he knows how to use it. It has already enabled him to cover the walls of his restaurant with photos of famous people eager to sit where the queen sat. In July 1995 signor Pagnani had a golden opportunity. Naples was to host the congress of the leaders of the seven most industrialized nations. While the mayor, signor Bassolino, was busy sprucing up Piazza del Plebiscito, signor Pagnani polished his powerful weapon and took aim. His target was the world's most influential men. The outcome was Piazza del Plebiscito emptied of cars and filled with an avalanche of fliers showing caricatures of the heads of government biting into a hot slice of Queen of Italy pizza and enthusing over its delicious taste. Headline: Brandi la pizza dei Grandi. The marketing operation soon bore its fruits and was especially effective with the younger generation. Today there is a new photo hanging up among the others in the pizzeria of the Queen of Italy. It portrays a smiling Chelsea Clinton embracing a triumphant Vincenzo Pagnani. She may not be a princess, but she's still a good catch.

Casa di S. M.

Capodimonte
11 Giugno 1889

Ispezione   Ufficio di Bocca

Pregiatissimo Sig. Raffaele Esposito Brandi
Le confermo che le tre qualità di Pizze
da Lei confezionate per Sua Maestà
la Regina vennero trovate buonissime
Mi creda di Lei

Devotissimo
G. Camillo
Capo dei Servizi di Tavola
della Real Casa

'A MARGARITA

'A QUANDO STA 'O BENESSERE
'A GENTE PENZA A SPENNERE
E MO' PURE 'O CHIÙ POVERO
'O SIENTE 'E CUMANNA';

VOGLIO UNA PIZZA A VONGOLE
CHIENA 'E FUNGHETTE E COZZECHE
CON GAMBERETTI E OSTRICHE
D'O MARE E STA CITTÀ.

AL CENTRO POI CE VOGLIO
N'UOVO FATTO ALLA COCCA
E CO LIGUORE STOK
L'AVITA ANNAFFIA'.

QUANDO SENTENNO ST'ORDINE
CE VENE CCA 'NA STIZZA
PENZANNO MA STI PIZZE,
SONGO PAPOCCHIE O CHE.

CA SE RISPETTA 'A REGOLA
FACENNO 'A VERA PIZZA
CHELLA CH'È NATA A NAPULE
QUASE CIENT'ANNE FA.

CHESTA RICETTA ANTICA
SI CHIAMMA MARGARITA
CA QUANNO È FATTA ARTE
PO GHÌ NANT' 'A NU RE.

PERCIÒ NUN E CERCATE
STI PIZZE COMPLICATE
CA FANNO MALE 'A SACCA,
E 'O STOMMACO PATÌ.

Poesia di G. ESPOSITO

Pizzas from 3,000 lire upwards. Pizzas from 4,000 lire upwards. Pizzas from 5,000 lire upwards.

In the De' Figliole pizzeria, speciality — deep-fried pizza, there's only the embarrassment of choosing!

From platter of the poor to whim of the wealthy

Pulcinella is the most famous Neapolitan mask and the one that best represents the Neapolitan spirit. There is a farce in which, by an odd twist of fate, Pulcinella becomes king and, realizing that the prestige of his new rank meant that he would have to stop eating pasta and pizza, exclaims: 'If that's the case, I'm going to un-king myself right now!' This quip is a perfect reflection of just how strong the relationship was between pizza and the Neapolitan populace.

In fact, like pasta, Neapolitan pizza was the child of hunger and imagination. In the 18th century, Naples underwent an intense population explosion becoming one of the most densely inhabited cities in Europe, with an increasing number of poor people who faced a serious problem – empty stomachs and empty pockets. Up until then, the diet of the Neapolitan population had mainly consisted of meat and vegetables. Suddenly there was a drastic shortage of these products. Neapolitan genius, stimulated by hunger, invented the first food product that was filling, nourishing and, most importantly, cheap – pasta. And yet, spaghetti and macaroni with oil and cheese, and later with *pummarola*, Neapolitan tomato sauce, didn't solve all the problems. It's easy to cook good pasta, but to serve it you need plates, plates and more plates. The plates have to be washed and water isn't free. And you need forks, too, because eating boiling spaghetti smothered in tomato sauce with your hands isn't everybody's cup of tea. What was needed was another stroke of genius, an idea that was cheap but tasty, quick to make but nourishing and easy to eat, standing up, on the street and with hands. And so, in answer to the needs of the poor, in the late 18th century, the Neapolitan pizza was born.

This brilliant invention, intended for the stomachs of the poor and starving, turned out to be delicious, but, precisely because of its humble origins and its shamelessly low cost, it was literally ignored by bourgeoisie and aristocracy alike. At this end of the social ladder, the menu was constellated by elaborate French dishes prepared by chefs who were introduced to the Royal Courts of Naples by Napoleon's army. When the French nobility left Naples in 1815, their chefs stayed on, finding employment with the local aristocracy. The people of Naples in dialect called them *munzù*, a corruption of *monsieur*. On one side was the *munzù*, on the other side taverns, macaroni and pizza. But people murmured and rumours were spread; news of the exquisite plebeian platter crept into the courts of the nobility. And thus it was the aristocrats who, from the great height of their privilege, first stooped to explore pizza in order to satisfy a lofty whim. Totally bypassing the tables of the rich bourgeoisie, pizza was, in fact, first tasted by the nobility and thus it began its long journey from the slums of

Naples to the tables of the whole world.

A predecessor to the real Neapolitan pizza made its first entrance into the Royal Court in the 17th century, as the Neapolitan chronicles of the era recount, thanks to Dorotea di Capua, Marchioness of Campolattaro. During a court ball, Dorotea di Capua, who was pregnant, had a sudden craving – she just had to have a pizza! Viceroy Don Pietro Giron, Duke of Ossuna, who, it was rumoured, had a soft spot for her, immediately procured one. We are not given to know exactly what type of pizza it was, nor who made it, but, since the episode took place before the appearance of tomatoes in Neapolitan cooking, it is reasonable to presume that it was a 'white pizza', typical of the times. This was, however, the sole incident of its kind until the following century, when Ferdinand I, the Bourbon King of the Two Sicilies, who loved the simple food of his people, regularly sneaked off incognito to the pizzeria run by Antonio Testa, known as *'Ntuono 'o pizzaiolo*, to eat his famous pizza.

In 1772, the king wanted his wife Marie Caroline of Austria to taste this delicious speciality and, since it was inconceivable for a queen to mingle with the plebs in a pizzeria, he summoned Antonio Testa to his palace at Capodimonte. Pizza's debut on the royal menu was harshly criticized by the Neapolitan aristocracy who found it scandalous for a king to eat lower-class food. Even the queen herself disapproved of her husband's wish for pizza to be included among the official court dishes. 'Ntuono got something out of it, though, because, after his trip to the palace, his pizzas went up to the outrageous price of two cents each. Pizzerias and the secrets of pizza-making were passed down from father to son. A more surprising discovery, however, is that passion for pizza is also hereditary. About 60 years later, Ferdinand II, the grandson of Ferdinand I, continued the family tradition of going

to the Testa pizzeria on Salita S. Teresa, strictly incognito, of course. If anything, his enthusiasm for these pizzas surpassed even his grandfather's and he decided to do something about it. He charged Domenico Testa, Antonio's son, with the task of overseeing the construction of a wood-fuelled pizza oven in the gardens of the Capodimonte palace.

Other Neapolitan pizza-eating monarchs can be found in the second half of the 19th century, and not only in Naples but in Sicily, for example. At that time, Palermo was the second most important town in the Kingdom of the Two Sicilies, whose capital was Naples, and was strongly influenced by the Neapolitan way of doing things. And that included their way of eating. The story goes that the Florios, a noble Sicilian family, once organized a banquet in honour of King Leopold of Belgium on the Sultana, their galley at anchor in the port of Palermo. Faced with a selection of elaborate Sicilian dishes and a Neapolitan pizza, apparently the monarch went straight for the pizza, of which he then took second helpings, much to the embarrassment of those present.

These episodes alone, however, were not enough to change the minds of the minor aristocracy and incorruptible bourgeoisie. In these circles, pizza was still spurned and considered strictly proletarian. The real turning point was the famous event of June 1889, featuring pizza Margherita and Queen Margherita of Italy. Although this wasn't the aristocracy's first experience of pizza, it was the first time that shook the bourgeoisie out of their complacency, breaking down their resistance. When they finally yielded to temptation, the consequences were inevitable – they loved it! And, whether they wanted to or not, they contributed to the diffusion of pizza among the middle classes. And so it was that the aroma of pizza from the lowest quarters of Neapolitan society finally wafted up to the higher echelons.

Totò is one of the most celebrated personalities of postwar Italian cinema. His childhood was spent in the backstreets of Naples. Totò brought all the character traits typical of his people to life on the silver screen – facial expressions, cunning and impertinence, as well as the art of the confidence trick, an example of which might explain the notice in this pizzeria which reads: 'Through the fault of one, credit to none.'

ZZERIA

DELLA

NA D'ITAL

Pizza fritta – deep-fried pizza – is a totally Neapolitan speciality which, despite its name, differs significantly from traditional Neapolitan pizza on two essential counts: its shape and how it is cooked. Like the 'calzone', or pizza with filling, it is folded over onto itself, and, instead of being baked in an oven, it is deep-fried in oil or lard in special pans. Although a favourite among connoisseurs, it isn't quite as light on the stomach as the traditional Neapolitan pizza and, to add insult to injury, in the rare pizzerias of Naples that still serve this old speciality, it is usually filled with ingredients that can be deemed anything but easy to digest: sausage and friarelli (a kind of broccoli), or ciccioli (scraps of pork fat), salame and ricotta, or even browned onions and mozzarella. And for dessert, deep-fried pizza with Nutella.

The dough

Flour, water, salt. Behind the blending of these three simple ingredients lies a story nearly as old as the history of man itself. A well-known Neapolitan writer, Luciano De Crescenzo, associates it with the very beginning of civilization. In fact, the cultivation of cereals coincides with a fundamental step in the history of man – the transition from nomadic to sedentary life. Primitive tribes stopped wandering from place to place in search of food when they noticed that, if they threw seeds on the ground, the seeds turned into wheat and the wheat produced more seeds. Man then soon got the hang of grinding the wheat and mixing it with water in order to obtain a kind of paste which, when cooked on scorching stones, was delicious. It was the start of a revolution that was to go through two more essential stages: the discovery of leavening and the invention of the oven, both of which were achieved by the Ancient Egyptians. The Egyptians were engaged in widespread corn farming, thanks to the favourable conditions resulting from the flooding of the Nile. Indeed, it would appear that the discovery of the process of natural fermentation was prompted by one of these floods.

Today we think that nothing could be more normal than the fact that, given the right temperature and humidity, a mixture of water, yeast and flour will gradually increase its volume. But what might have been the reaction of that Ancient Egyptian who, on returning to his larder, found that his much-beloved cracker had turned into a roll, all thanks to the particular degree of humidity created by the flooding of the Nile?
Did he calmly explain to his incredulous friends that micro-organisms called yeasts had probably attacked

the carbohydrates in the flour and produced molecules of gas which, in all likelihood, had made the mixture bigger, softer and more acidulous? Or did he run all over the place shouting out that he had just witnessed some incredible magic? In the more plausible event of the second hypothesis, once he had recovered from the shock, maybe our Ancient Egyptian was tempted to try and cook this magically leavened dough. And, perhaps, unaware of the significance of his new discovery, he made the first loaf of leavened bread in history.

In the mixture for the Neapolitan pizza of today, the leavening process may be instigated by adding either natural or artificial yeast. The former is simply a small amount of the dough left over from the day before, mixed with more flour, water and salt. This is the system most commonly used by Neapolitan pizza-makers. Vincenzo Pagnani, pizza-maker since he was 14 years old and owner of the famous Brandi pizzeria in Via Sant'Anna di Palazzo, is a firm supporter of the old school leavening technique. 'Otherwise the pizza grows in your stomach,' he says. Not everybody agrees, however, and in many pizzerias in Naples you can enjoy excellent pizzas made with baker's yeast. Apart from yeast, be it of the natural variety or baker's yeast, and apart from white, plain flour obtained from soft wheat, the other pizza dough ingredient is water.

Why is pizza better in Naples? The local inhabitants proudly claim that the secret lies in the water of the Serino aqueduct, so unmistakably soft and light, the same water that was sold by Neapolitan *acquaiuoli* in the 19th century in earthenware jars, and which is still today more thirst-quenching than any beer or wine.

A little scepticism is more than legitimate considering that the Serino aqueduct, which carries water from an excellent spring in the province of Avellino, only serves a very small part of the modern city. And yet there must be some truth in the legend of the water of Naples, if water has anything to do with the undeniable fact that there is no other place in the world where they serve a cup of coffee as irresistibly smooth and rich. With or without the Serino water, it is nevertheless essential that the pizza-maker use lukewarm water (approximately 28°C/82°F) in precise doses taking the humidity in the atmosphere into account, if the dough is to have the correct degree of elasticity.

Neapolitan pizza-makers in action are a spectacular sight, as they roll the dough, tossing it into the air with the confidence of accomplished acrobats, making it thinner and wider with each movement until it turns into a splendid round disc. This ritual, which is as old as the Neapolitan pizza itself, is much more than a mere display of manual skill. The Neapolitan pizza-maker is well aware of the fact that, by using the centrifugal force generated by rotating the dough, he will end up with a disc that is perfectly round, of ideal thickness and with that much sought-after border that Neapolitans call the *cornicione*. This border, which is no more than a couple of centimetres (¾in) wide and never has any topping, has a fundamental role in the Neapolitan pizza – it turns the pizza into a container, preventing the oil and other ingredients from running off the surface of the dough when the pizza-maker moves the pizza around in the oven with his baker's shovel and takes it out for serving. Today the delicious and masterly *cornicione* is often neglected by pizza-eaters pressed for time, who leave it on the side of their plates after gulping down the middle of their pizza. And yet, Salvatore Di Giacomo, in the daily newspaper *Corriere di Napoli* in 1893, tells of a father who, in a period of economic hardship, in order to feed his family, reached an agreement with his local pizza-maker who kept the left-over *cornicioni* for him every evening.

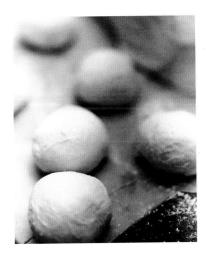

The wood oven

More than the tomato or mozzarella, more than the fresh basil or oregano, what really distinguishes an authentic Neapolitan pizza is the unmistakable, unique aroma of the oven it is cooked in. The wood-fuelled oven is, in fact, an essential factor in the creation of a genuine Neapolitan pizza. Whereas in pizzerias all over the world electric ovens are rapidly replacing wood ovens, in Naples, wood ovens, with their colourful decorations, are the pride and joy of every pizza-maker in town.

The first oven in history appeared in Ancient Egypt. Once the Ancient Egyptians had discovered the phenomenon of leavening, there was no stopping in their quest for a decent loaf of bread. Bored of the same old flat bread baked on hot rocks, they invented a system for enclosing fire for cooking purposes, making rudimental ovens that gradually became more sophisticated in the form of a cylinder or cone, with two sections inside – underneath went the fire, on top the dough. As time passed, of course, some of the original Ancient Egyptian design features were slightly modified.

In fact, traditional Neapolitan pizza ovens are dome-shaped; their ceilings are heated by direct contact with the flames of the wood fire laid on the floor of the oven, i.e. not below but on the cooking surface. This design, which ensures that the heat is distributed evenly, is at least 2,000 years old. Excavations at Pompeii, just outside Naples, have brought to light dome-shaped ovens used for baking bread. So, behind the expert use of the wood oven by Neapolitan pizza-makers and even behind the very construction of these ovens lies a score of secrets that have been passed down through the centuries. Some important clues to how the ovens are made can be found in Maiano, a village not far from Naples with little more than a handful of houses and as many families, all or most of whom

bear the same surname, Aversa. Here, bricks for wood ovens have been manufactured according to traditional methods which have been passed down from father to son for over five centuries; since the 15th century, special hand-made bricks have been produced by working the clay in the Sorrento peninsula with time-honoured techniques. As the Code of the *Vera Pizza Napoletana* states, the inside of wood ovens must be entirely lined with special heat-resistant fire-bricks.

In Neapolitan pizzerias, the fire in the oven never goes out completely. Even when there are no pizzas in the oven, the burning embers keep the temperature high; then, when it is time to cook the pizzas, the oven reaches approximately 400°C (752°F). At this temperature, pizza cooks quickly, in 80 to 90 seconds, the tomato dehydrates to exactly the right degree, the basil doesn't lose its aroma, the mozzarella melts without overthickening and the fatty acids of the olive oil don't alter their structure. The pizza cooks directly on the oven floor, not in baking tins, and the oven is fed with types of wood that don't smoke very much as they burn, like cherry or olive wood, and shavings. And this is the secret of that light but wonderful oven flavour.

Anyone who has eaten a pizza made in an authentic Neapolitan wood oven will confirm that there is much more to making pizza in wood-fuelled ovens than mere folklore; that subtle smoky fragrance, always perceptible and never too much, that invisible veil of ash that inevitably clings to the bottom of the doughy disc, the burned crispness of the border – all this is the result of techniques of which only Neapolitan pizza-makers are the real masters, techniques that come from centuries of experience. No sport can boast a team spirit equal to that of the pizza-maker and his assistant, as they celebrate the most magical moment of the pizza rite.

Once the pizza-maker has finished putting the topping on the pizza base, with a simple glance or a thunderous call in Neapolitan dialect, he asks his assistant for the baker's shovel. The assistant grabs a wooden shovel, a large one for putting things in the oven, and moves it close to the work surface. The pizza-maker sprinkles it with flour and lays the pizza on it, if necessary giving the pizza a little tug to stretch it out. Once the shovel has been introduced into the oven, the pizza is tossed off with a single, sharp jerk which, by some unfathomable mystery, propels it safely and intact onto the oven floor.

The dome-shaped surface inside the oven is white from the heat of the wood burning on a bed of embers on one side of the oven, and the scorching air causes the border of the pizza to rise within a few seconds. The pizza-maker grabs another shovel, a small, metal one, and pours a shovelful of shavings onto the fire which instantly flares up. At this stage, the pizza-maker embarks upon a series of apparently casual movements with the small shovel; in reality, he is meticulously calibrating the distance between the pizza and the fire, moving it closer, rotating it and shifting it further away, until it is ready for removal from the oven. About one and a half minutes have passed since the pizza was put in. This is the time it takes to perform the true rite of the genuine Neapolitan pizza.

Ferdinand I, King of Two Sicilies, visited the pizzeria of Antonio Testa, known as 'Ntuono 'o pizzaiuolo, to try the dish about which he had heard so much. He was so delighted by the pizza's succulent flavours that he invited 'Ntuono to court, so that he could make a pizza for the queen, Maria Carolina. Since they didn't have a proper pizza oven at court, the story goes that the pizza-maker was obliged to avail himself of the much more powerful ovens used for firing the famous Capodimonte porcelain. It seems a safe guess that the first court pizzas were a little overdone. Ferdinand II, 63 years later, decided to follow in the footsteps of his grandfather and went incognito to the Testa family pizzeria now run by Domenico, 'Ntuono's son. Here, he tasted the legendary pizza and he immediately employed Domenico to make a pizza oven in the park of the Reggia di Capodimonte. In no time at all there was a royal brick oven big enough to cook seven pizzas at once.

Tomatoes

Alexandre Dumas, creator of *The Three Musketeers* and *The Count of Monte Cristo*, spent a few days in Naples in 1835. In his book of memoirs, he lists the pizzas then available in Naples: with olive oil, with lard, with small fish (the almost extinct pizza *ai cecinielli*), with cheese and with tomato. This is one of the first-recorded references to pizza topped with tomato, even though tomatoes had been around in Europe for over three centuries. They came to the old world from Peru, courtesy of Christopher Columbus, but when they finally reached Europe, they didn't head straight for the kitchen. Tomatoes in those days were, of course, very different to their modern counterparts. They were the size of cherries, yellow and, probably, much sharper tasting. Up until then, they had been grown in Peru for ornamental purposes only. In Europe, the tomato plant was imported as a botanical rarity. In 1640, Cardinal Richelieu was given four of them as a gift from the aristocracy of Toulon, and in France, throughout the 17th century, twigs of tomato were presented to noble young ladies by hopeful suitors as a token of their love. At the time, tomatoes were also believed to be an aphrodisiac. This is why the first names for tomato in Europe referred to love – *pomme d'amour* in French, love apple in English and *Liebelsapfel* in German.

The Italians were the first to include tomatoes in their recipes. In 1696, a German author wrote that 'the Italians have even been known to eat the fruit of this plant although it is unhealthy and harmful'. It was only in the late 18th and early 19th centuries, however, that tomato cultivation really began, especially in the area between Naples and Salerno, providing Neapolitan pizza-makers with a product that was no longer imported and, therefore, inexpensive. So they turned white pizzas, hitherto made with lard and cheese, into the red, tomato-topped variety, and the true Neapolitan pizza, as we know it today, was born.

In America new varieties of this now typically Mediterranean vegetable are continually being produced, so much so that there are over 5,000 kinds of tomato in the world today. But, beware, you can't just

Because of the tomato's high solanin content, for a long time it was thought to be poisonous. Legend would have it that Abraham Lincoln's chef, in a dastardly plot to undo the president, tried to poison him by serving him a dish garnished with tomato.

put any old tomato on a Neapolitan pizza. In fact, if you want to respect the authentic Neapolitan tradition, only one type of tomato is acceptable – the San Marzano, with its instantly recognizable light-bulb shape, grown in an area stretching from the slopes of Vesuvius to the temples of Paestum. Once, beside every Neapolitan pizza oven, there was always a bunch of tomatoes *a chiummenza*, as they say in Naples, i.e. hanging from a nail in the wall, as was the custom in people's homes. Today more and more often fresh tomatoes are replaced by convenient cans of peeled tomatoes (the tomatoes are scalded, peeled, slightly salted and canned), or by canned chopped tomatoes, a natural, high-quality, easy-to-use product which is now quite popular with Neapolitan pizza-makers.

The Naples area is famous the world over for its important tomato-processing industry. Here, in 'tomato-land', everything seems to revolve round this sun-drenched vegetable. From confirmations to weddings, everything is put off till summer, when the tomato harvest provides a large proportion of the population with work and enough income to get by for the rest of the year. And so, thanks to this flourishing local industry, tomatoes, whether hanging up beside the oven or preserved in cans, peeled or chopped, take the lead role in every pizzeria. Note, however, that professional pizza-makers steer clear of tomato purée which tends to blunt the flavours, making all pizzas taste the same. Moreover, they always put the tomato directly onto the dough, before the mozzarella, because otherwise the starch in the dough would mix with the mozzarella proteins in the oven, making the pizza a little heavy on the stomach. Because tomatoes are 94 per cent water, pizza-makers always make sure that they are drained of surplus water, whether using fresh, peeled or chopped tomatoes, to avoid the risk of soggy dough.

The legendary San Marzano tomatoes are cultivated uniquely in the area around Naples that extends from the slopes of Vesuvius to the temples of Paestum. The ancient custom that unites families after the festival of Ferragosto in mid-August for the traditional tomato-bottling rite is still very much alive today. It is hard work, but also a truly joyful occasion involving the whole family, parents and children alike, whose final reward is the pulp of the world's most famous peeled tomato.

Mozzarella

Pure buffalo milk and the art of the dairyman. Put the two together in Campania, the region of Naples, and you get the most famous Italian cheese in the world. Exceptional softness, peculiar elasticity, that distinctive tang and the white teardrop rolling down the blade of the knife as it is sliced — all these things make it impossible to mistake any other cheese for genuine mozzarella. And once you have tried the real thing, you will be happy to join the club of fussy restaurant-goers who always ask for the waiter's complete assurance that, in his establishment, they only use genuine buffalo-milk mozzarella.

Really there shouldn't be any need to specify, since mozzarella has always exclusively meant buffalo-milk cheese. The confusion arises because, after the Second World War, the demand for mozzarella grew while the buffalo population decreased, and so production began of a similar cheese following the mozzarella method but with cow's milk. Mozzarella-like cheese made of cow's milk is called, or should be called, '*fior di latte*'. In fact, a legal battle is currently being fought in Italy over the right to use the term 'mozzarella'.

Producers of the pure buffalo-milk variety want to stop the term being used by producers of similar cheeses made with cow's milk or a combination of cow and buffalo milk. But real mozzarella is and will always be the variety made with pure buffalo milk in the traditional, officially recognized production areas in Italy which comprise most of Campania, and parts of Latium and Apulia.

Since this was the only type of mozzarella in existence when the inhabitants of Naples were happily inventing the pizza, the tradition requires that only buffalo-milk mozzarella be used, and it is universally recognized as having more flavour than *fior di latte*. The fact is, though, that Neapolitan pizza-makers do not all agree. Traditionalists insist that cow's milk mozzarella-like cheese is totally unacceptable, but another school of thought maintains that the excessive milkiness of buffalo-milk mozzarella can spoil the texture of the dough. This is why, for example, they only serve pizzas with *fior di latte* at Brandi's, the pizzeria of Queen Margherita fame. The belligerent pizza-makers have reached a truce, thanks to the *Associazione Vera Pizza Napoletana*, whose Code allows both kinds of mozzarella. And perhaps, when all is said and done, the truth is that, while pizza Margherita made with real buffalo-milk mozzarella is unbeatable and inimitable, other more elaborate kinds of pizza with more ingredients on them improve with the less fatty *fior di latte*.

The origin of the Italian buffalo is far from clear. The most plausible theory is that the Longobards brought buffaloes to Italy with them during the descent of the Barbarians in the 6th and 7th centuries AD, as the historian Paul the Deacon recounts in his *Historia Longobardorum*. After a long and adventurous journey, these buffaloes settled in the marshlands which then stretched from Paestum to the Gulf of Salerno, whose humid climate was to their liking. Still today there is something ancestral about watching these immense animals sinking gracefully into the water to cool down and escape from the heat of the scorching Mediterranean sun.

Even establishing the origin of mozzarellas is tricky. Some claim that in the area known as Campania today mozzarellas were already being produced at the time of Ancient Rome, when southern Italy was called Magna Grecia. One thing is certain – this famous cheese was made long before its first mention in historical documents. The term *mozza* first appears in a document in the Episcopal Archives of the Church of Capua, which dates back only to the 12th century. And the currently used dimunitive form *mozzarella* turns up for the first time in *Opera Culinaria*, published in 1570 by a chef in the employ of the Pope, one Bartolomeo Scappi, known as Il Platina. The name 'mozzarella' is derived from the verb *mozzare*, which means 'to cut off', referring to a critical stage at the heart of the mozzarella production process. In fact, this process, an art at which the Campania dairymen really excel, involves seven separate stages, from milking the buffalo to the immersion of the mozzarella in brine to give it the right flavour. But the name refers to the precise moment when the curdled milk breaks and becomes stringy. In this instant, the mozzarella begins to take shape and a helper grabs large chunks of it and passes them to the dairyman who 'cuts off' the right amount to make a single mozzarella, which can vary in weight from 70g (2½oz) for the tiny one-mouthful globes of cheese known as *bocconcini* to 600g (1lb 5oz) for the plaited mozzarella known as *treccia*.

Generally speaking, the *treccia* is the type with the strongest flavour and the *bocconcino* is the most delicate. However, in mozzarella folklore, the moon is also an important factor in determining the final flavour. Allegedly, the taste of the buffalo milk undergoes the influence of the lunar cycle and the best mozzarella is made after the animals have grazed during nights when the moon is full. As with all legends, there is an element of truth in this one, too. Atmospheric conditions do affect the taste of mozzarella, and this is why it is better not put it in the fridge. Ideally, mozzarella should be kept at a constant room temperature and eaten as fresh as possible, swimming in its own whey.

Basil

The first taste that springs to mind when one thinks of Mediterranean cuisine is the strong, emphatic flavour of olive oil, just as its dominant colour is the bright red of ripe tomatoes. But there can be little doubt that its most representative aroma is the pert, sharp scent of the freshly picked basil leaf. Indeed, it is no coincidence that the Code regulating the true Neapolitan pizza states that 'all varieties of pizza appreciate a basil leaf or two'. Tomato and basil provide such a harmonious merger of flavour and colour that they must have been made for each other. And what better nuptial bed for them to celebrate their union than the pizza?

Basil originally came from Persia, but was already grown all over Asia and the Middle East 4,000 years ago. It did not reach Europe, however, until the 1st century BC, when it was introduced by the Romans, and today it is still cultivated all round the Mediterranean.

It is handy to know that basil grows well in a pot. If you plant a few plants in spring, you will have a fresh supply of leaves for the whole summer. You can put basil in the freezer for winter, although this tends to give the flavour a slightly minty edge. Growing basil may be fairly straightforward, but the same cannot be said about its correct use. There are three important points to bear in mind in order not spoil the aroma. First of all basil should be picked by snapping the leaves off the plants with the fingers; for the same reason, it should not be washed in water, but gently brushed with a tea-towel; and lastly, it should be added just before the pizza is removed from the oven, because excessive exposure to high temperatures gives it a bitter taste.

The idea that basil leaves should be picked by hand and not cut with a knife comes from one of the many legends surrounding this plant. The legend says that basil benefits from contact with human hands. And maybe this was one of the reasons why it was once customary among aristocrats to caress basil plants in order to have the scent on their hands. Basil has always, effectively, been much loved by the nobility. Starting with its name, which derives from *basilikòs*, a Greek term for regal, basil was the king of herbs, cultivated by court attendants and used to make ointments for the king himself.

But basil has enjoyed the favour of the aristocracy in more recent times, too. Let it not be forgotten that it was thanks to this regal herb that in 1889 the Neapolitan pizza-maker, Don Raffaele Esposito, won the favour of a queen, when, summoned to court in order to present his pizzas to Margherita of Savoy, the queen so appreciated the union of basil with mozzarella and tomato that she agreed to associating her name with the three-coloured pizza for ever.

Garlic

No food in the ancient world was more popular than garlic, or so it seems. Through the centuries, garlic was thought to have many different hidden properties or magical effects and, in particular, it became a symbol of the powers that protect man against evil. In the *Odyssey*, for example, the god Hermes shields Ulysses from the sorceress Circe's filters by getting him to eat some.

The Ancient Egyptians were the first to grow garlic. Since the plant was associated with the cult of Sokar, the god of the underworld, the pharaohs were not allowed to eat it, but, aware of its nutritious qualities, they gave it to their slaves in generous doses to fortify them for the construction of the pyramids. The Romans also believed in garlic's ability to invigorate the human body and, therefore, consecrated it to Mars, the god of war. Nero's doctor prescribed garlic and honey for the Emperor's voice. For the Celts, garlic was a symbol of virility. Henry IV was extremely keen on it and perhaps this is why he went down in history as a great lover. During his baptism, garlic was rubbed on his tongue to make him strong and healthy. In the Middle Ages, garlic was appreciated for its anti-Satanic properties – it was woven into necklaces which were worn or hung near doors to ward off evil spirits. During the Renaissance, garlic was significantly less popular both with the masses and at court, because of its rather distinct odour.

And today? Although they are few and far between, popular beliefs associated with garlic still survive. In some villages in Sicily, for example, bunches of garlic placed on the beds of women about to give birth bring good luck. All sorts of beneficial effects and therapeutic properties are still attributed to garlic, as can be seen from the number of herbal remedies containing it. But garlic really reigns supreme in the kitchen, where it plays a fundamental role. It comes as no surprise, then, to find this typical ingredient of Mediterranean cuisine in all traditional Neapolitan dishes, on bruschetta, with fish, in pasta sauces and, of course, on pizza – and in particular the simple but wonderfully tasty pizza Marinara. Thinly sliced or chopped into tiny pieces, garlic should, nevertheless, be used sparingly on pizzas; its flavour should not drown the other ingredients, but should mix in with them harmoniously. At all costs, avoid garlic that has been hanging around the kitchen too long. Garlic is best fresh and the best garlic comes from places with hot climates, especially the area around the Mediterranean. Here, it is picked in summer and left to dry for at least a week in hot, ventilated places. Then it is bunched or plaited and hung up. At this stage it is ready for consumption, and the sooner you use it, the better your pizza will be.

On account of its often bemoaned 'smell', the Ancient Greeks referred to garlic as 'rank rose'. Perhaps they didn't know there are several good ways to mitigate the negative effects that garlic can have on close encounters of every possible kind. Here are a few hints: slowly chew on coffee beans for a few minutes; if you are right out of coffee beans, parsley, aniseed, fennel, artichoke leaves or juniper berries will do; alternatively, eat grated apples or the odd teaspoon of honey. A tip for those prone to indigestion: don't eat the green 'eye' – it is the least digestible part of the clove; the flavour is unaffected.

Olive oil

Olive trees have been around for over 3,000 years and are the oldest type of fruit tree in the world. While the Ancient Greeks considered the olive tree as holy and, in some regions, cutting one down was punishable by death, for the Romans, the olive tree was a symbol of peace and victory – on their return from battle, victorious generals were garlanded with olive wreaths. For the Hebrews, the first olive tree sprouted on Adam's grave from a seed that was given to his son Seth by an angel of Paradise. A symbol of rebirth and renewal, an olive branch was brought to Noah by the dove announcing the first piece of dry land to emerge out of the Flood. Even Christianity, despite its lengthy battle against pagan tree cults, had a soft spot for the olive tree. It became a symbol of peace, and still today, in the Catholic rite on Palm Sunday, olive branches are blessed and taken home.

Today over 90 per cent of the world's olive trees are cultivated in the Mediterranean basin. But why is it that the peoples of this area have been assigning divine properties to olive trees since ancient times? The answer probably lies in the relationship of olive oil both to the earth and to the labour of man. As from the vine we get wine and from corn we get bread, so from the olive tree nature and man create olive oil.

Although over the centuries little or nothing has changed in the way olive oil is produced, the same cannot be said of the way it is perceived. Olive oil had to wait patiently until the Seventies before finally and triumphantly winning the battle against butter. Statistics showed that, beyond doubt, health problems typical of prosperous butter-consuming northern nations, such as heart disease, were much less frequent in the humble oil-consuming Mediterranean countries. From then on, olive oil's well-deserved popularity has been spreading like wildfire. In fact, olive oil is the most natural and easiest fat for us to digest, and what's more, it aids the digestion of other fats. So, there is more to olive oil than mere salad dressing. It is a complete food in its own right.

The best type of olive oil is called *vergine* (virgin). This is the only variety produced without chemical manipulation. Among the 'virgin' oils, the so-called *extra-vergine* type has the lowest acidity of all. It costs a little more, but it's money well spent. Whereas other oils form harmful substances at high temperatures, the extra-virgin variety resists heat, which is why it is the only type allowed on Neapolitan pizzas. The Neapolitan pizza-maker is, nevertheless, well aware of the fact that it should not be exposed to the high temperature of the pizza oven for more than 90 seconds, otherwise the structure of its precious fatty acids could be altered. The ideal quantity should not exceed 10g (¼oz), otherwise the flavour of the olive oil could overshadow the other tastes. And here is his secret – after arranging all the other ingredients on the disc, the pizza-maker adds the oil by artistically drawing a figure of six with an *agliara*, a traditional Neapolitan oil-cruet with a tapered spout. This way he is sure he has poured the right amount.

The way in which oil is extracted from olives has not changed much over the centuries. Today most of the production takes place in smallish mills and grindstones are still usually made of granite, just as they used to be. Olives are harvested around November and, once impurities have been removed, they are crushed in presses. The result is a pulp made up of oil, water, pith, skin and the stone. The oil is separated from this pulp centrifugally and by decanting, and has to rest for several months at a temperature of 15°C (59°F) before being bottled.

Pizza taboos

Pizza with fried eggs, figs and bananas, pizza with Nutella, pizza with fennel, paprika and frankfurters.... A quick glance at the menu of one of the thousands of pizzerias on our planet and it would appear that there is no limit to the imagination where pizza is concerned. And yet, Neapolitan pizza, is subject to a series of extremely rigorous restrictions.

In reaction to this unlimited and limitless production of pizzas that are anything but the genuine Neapolitan article, the *Associazione Vera Pizza Napoletana* (Real Neapolitan Pizza Association) was set up in Naples. Members of the Association consist of pizzerias committed to making pizza according to the rules laid out in a Code, which regulates cooking procedure and raw materials. In fact, the main purpose of the Association is to defend the original version against imitations, to defend Neapolitan pizza against any old pizza.

According to the Association, the vast category of the thing called pizza is basically divided into three kinds: pizza Napoletana, pizza alla Napoletana and others. Apart from the truly original Neapolitan pizza, Marinara or Margherita, the Code permits variations as long as they are in keeping with the spirit of the great tradition and don't contravene the rules of good taste and gastronomy. All the rest simply isn't Naples – and, ergo, isn't real pizza.

The bad habit of considering pizza as a kind of container to be topped according to the whim of the moment is by no means a recent phenomenon. The first official recipe for a pizza appeared in 1858 in a book by Emmanuele Rocco, significantly entitled *Usi e costumi di Napoli e Contorni* [Usages and Customs of Naples and Surrounds]. It reads: 'Take a piece of dough, make it larger and stretch it with a rolling pin or beat it by hand, put on top of it whatever takes your fancy, add oil or lard, cook it in an oven and you will discover what pizza is'.

Luckily for signor Rocco, the Code of the *Associazione Vera Pizza Napoletana* didn't exist in 1858. But with respect to all the pizzerias in existence today, in every corner of the Earth including Naples, that continue to serve pizza à la leftover, with toppings that consist of whatever's at the back of the fridge, the rules are inflexible. They will never be allowed to display the much sought-after symbol of the Association.

So how do you make real Neapolitan pizza? The Code of the *Associazione Vera Pizza Napoletana*

Strawberry jam, vanilla ice-cream and kiwi, spread on a sweet disc of pastry. It is not always easy to tell real Neapolitan pizza from its imitations.

sets out strict and unequivocal rules for making pizza; and it's enough to break just one of them to jeopardize the authenticity of your pizza beyond repair.

Here is a list of genuine Neapolitan pizza taboos, extrapolated from the official rules. The Code leaves no room for doubt. It is taboo to:
• use fat in the dough – real Neapolitan pizza must be made exclusively from flour, natural or brewer's yeast, salt and water;
• use a rolling pin – the dough must be kneaded manually or with special pizza-kneading devices approved by the Association;
• use a baking tin – pizzas must be cooked directly on the oven floor;
• use an electric oven – only wood-fuelled, bell-shaped ovens whose sides are made of fire-bricks and fire-clay and whose floors are made of special refractory material are allowed;
• fuel the fire artificially – only pieces of wood and wood shavings may be burnt.
These impositions may be a little daunting, but the Code guarantees that, when rigorously followed, the reward is deeply gratifying – your pizza will be 'supple, perfectly cooked, fragrant and framed by a high, soft border'.

The real importance of all these rules may not be immediately obvious to a non-Neapolitan. For pizza in Naples is so much more than a wholesome, delicious, cheap meal; so much more than the symbol of a city and the creativity of its inhabitants. Performed on a daily basis in the pizzerias and in the piazza, in side-streets and on the kerbstone, it is a rite whose every step, from preparation to consumption, respects the old tradition. In fact, leaving aside the written rules, Neapolitan pizza is surrounded by an aura of uncodified, unforced rules, dictated by nobody in particular but deriving from a series of gestures, rituals and habits that have, through the centuries, become an integral part of Neapolitan culture.

Nevertheless, when the puzzled outsider sets foot inside a pizzeria, suddenly all becomes clear. Eaten within the unadorned walls of a traditional Neapolitan pizzeria, between the white wall tiles and the white flour on the work surface where the pizzas are created in everybody's view, at one of a handful of tables made of wood or marble, in earshot of the crackling wood in the pizza oven, the exclamations of the pizza-maker and his assistant's colourful retorts in Neapolitan dialect, pizza tastes unforgettably different.

In Naples, everyone has an opinion on pizza and his or her secret. So it would appear that another huge taboo is cold pizza. In the pizzeria, the number one enemy is time. A gentleman from Capri recommended ordering pizzas at intervals and sharing each pizza as it arrived among the diners so that everyone would have it hot from the first to the last slice. The famous Neapolitan actor and film director Vittorio De Sica always asked for a table near the oven so that his pizza wouldn't get cold on its voyage from oven to table.

And then, in Naples, there are those who prefer to eat pizza with their hands, like in the old days. Hence the pizza *a libretto*, or folded pizza, served in the Pizzeria Di Matteo, in Via dei Tribunali, in the historical town centre, which is always packed at lunchtime. The pizza is folded into four pieces, hot and ready to be eaten hand-held and in the street. Everybody indulges, from youngsters perched on their Vespa to distinguished ladies careful not to stain their business suits. Even President Clinton indulged on a visit to Naples. And judging by the satisfied expression on his face in the photograph on the pizzeria wall, he loved it!

And that's without mentioning Gigino and his famous pizzeria in Vico Equense on the peninsula of Sorrento, just outside Naples. This is the man who invented pizza by the metre. It was back in the Fifties when Gigino dared to challenge the time-honoured tradition by being the first to produce long, rectangular pizzas instead of the classic round articles. He then sold them by cutting them according to request. So it was that a broken taboo, regarding pizza shape, not only made the fortune of Gigino at Vico Equense, but started off an entire new trend in pizzerias all over the world.

Recipes

Some hints. On the following pages, there are 28 recipes for pizza, all based on the disc of dough made by the traditional Neapolitan method. Here are some tips that apply to most, if not all, of them.

For pizza recipes with tomato, the Neapolitan tradition would expect you to use the San Marzano variety, but if you can't readily get hold of authentic San Marzanos, any other Italian tomatoes with the same elongated shape or cherry tomatoes will do fine. Alternatively, bottled tomato pulp may be used. Never use tomato purée. Before you spread tomato over the pizza, remember to drain off as much moisture as you can, to avoid the dough becoming soggy.

If you opt for fresh tomatoes, make sure they are ripe. Fully ripened tomatoes lose their sharpness and all the subtleties of their flavour come out; moreover, they are easier to digest, so we can better assimilate the precious vitamins and minerals they contain.

For recipes with mozzarella, the Neapolitan tradition requires buffalo-milk mozzarella, which is more delicate and less compact than the cow's-milk variety. If you prefer your cheese less milky, cow's-milk mozzarella, known as *fior di latte* in Naples, is a valid alternative as long as it is fresh and full of flavour.

Basil must, of course, be fresh and aromatic. When cleaning basil, never use water, but brush it delicately with a light cloth.

If you do not have access to a special bread or pizza-baking oven, place a large baking or pizza stone or an unglazed terracotta tile in the middle of your electric or gas oven before heating. The pizza can either be baked directly on the stone or tile, or in a pizza pan or baking sheet, brushed lightly with olive oil, placed on top. This will ensure a crisp crust.

It is essential to put the pizza in a hot oven. Approximately 275°C (525°F) is the recommended temperature, but many conventional electric and gas ovens do not have the capacity to reach this high heat. In this case, preheat the oven to its highest temperature – usually 240°C (475°F) Gas Mark 9 – at least half an hour before baking and increase the baking times given in the recipes by approximately 5–8 minutes, if necessary. Remove the pizza when it is well cooked all over, but not burnt. Don't forget that pizza should be well cooked underneath, too. Check to make sure that the edge of the pizza doesn't turn too dark a colour. If there is mozzarella on the pizza, it should melt, but be careful not to burn it.

And remember... pizzas must be eaten hot, straight out of the oven. *Buon appetito!*

Dough

This quantity of dough is for four pizzas.

25G (1OZ) FRESH YEAST
250ML (9FL OZ) LUKEWARM WATER
400G (14OZ) UNBLEACHED STRONG PLAIN FLOUR
1 TSP SALT

1. Begin by making a yeast liquid. Dissolve the yeast in 25ml (1½ tablespoons) of the lukewarm water. Add about 2 tablespoons of the flour. Mix to a smooth paste. Leave to rise under a cloth for 30 minutes.
2. Make a crater with about 350g (12oz) of the flour (save the rest for the final kneading), with as deep a hole as possible in the middle. Pour the yeast liquid, salt and the rest of the water into the hole. Work the ingredients together carefully with well-floured hands. Knead continuously for about 10 minutes. When the dough is elastic, form it into a loaf and then cut it into 4 pieces of the same size. Form the pieces into balls and leave them to rise under a cloth for about 2 hours or until they have doubled in size.
3. Use one ball for one pizza. Knead for a couple of minutes. Press out and flatten the dough with the palm of your hand into a thin, round circle. Use a rolling pin to make it really thin. Finally, press with your knuckles about 2cm (¾in) inside the edge to make the raised edge (*cornicione*). The pizza is now ready to be filled.

Pizza Marinara

This is the original – simple and full of flavour.

RECIPE FOR A PIZZA FOR ONE PERSON.

START WITH THE DOUGH ON PAGE 122. DIVIDE THE DOUGH INTO FOUR AND USE ONE PIECE FOR EACH PERSON
OVEN TEMPERATURE: 275°C (525°F) – SEE PAGE 121
BAKING TIME: ABOUT 10-12 MINUTES – SEE PAGE 121

200G (7OZ) TOMATOES OF ONE OF THE FOLLOWING SORT:
CHERRY TOMATOES, CUT INTO HALVES
SAN MARZANO TOMATOES OR SIMILAR ITALIAN PLUM TOMATOES, CUT LENGTHWISE INTO 5MM (¼IN) SLICES
WHOLE CANNED TOMATOES, CRUSHED BY HAND AND DRAINED

1 CLOVE GARLIC, THINLY SLICED
1 TSP DRIED OREGANO
ABOUT 2 TBSP EXTRA-VIRGIN OLIVE OIL, PREFERABLY ITALIAN
SALT

1. Always let the tomatoes drain thoroughly before use to prevent the pizza from becoming soggy.
Drain canned tomatoes in a colander. Fresh tomatoes need some help. Put the sliced tomatoes into a colander and press them gently with your fist to remove as much moisture as possible.
2. Roll out the dough into a circle with a slightly thicker edge (*cornicione*). Spread the tomatoes evenly over the dough, but leave the edge (about 2cm/³⁄₄in) without tomato. Spread the garlic and sprinkle the oregano over the tomatoes. Sprinkle the pizza generously with olive oil and season with salt. Bake in the centre of the oven.

Pizza Margherita

The queen of pizzas.

RECIPE FOR A PIZZA FOR ONE PERSON.

START WITH THE DOUGH ON PAGE 122. DIVIDE THE DOUGH INTO FOUR AND USE ONE PIECE FOR EACH PERSON
OVEN TEMPERATURE: 275°C (525°F) – SEE PAGE 121
BAKING TIME: ABOUT 10–12 MINUTES – SEE PAGE 121

200G (7OZ) TOMATOES OF ONE OF THE FOLLOWING SORT:
CHERRY TOMATOES, CUT INTO HALVES
SAN MARZANO TOMATOES OR SIMILAR ITALIAN PLUM TOMATOES, CUT LENGTHWISE INTO 5MM (¼IN) SLICES
WHOLE CANNED TOMATOES, CRUSHED BY HAND AND DRAINED

50G (1¾OZ) MOZZARELLA (THE ORIGINAL MADE FROM BUFFALO MILK) OR *FIOR DI LATTE* (MOZZARELLA MADE FROM COW'S MILK), SLICED
5–6 FRESH BASIL LEAVES
SALT
ABOUT 1 TBSP EXTRA-VIRGIN OLIVE OIL, PREFERABLY ITALIAN

1. Always let the tomatoes drain thoroughly before use to prevent the pizza from becoming soggy. Drain canned tomatoes in a colander. Fresh tomatoes need some help. Put the sliced tomatoes into a colander and press them gently with your fist to remove as much moisture as possible. The same applies to mozzarella made from buffalo milk. Put the mozzarella slices into a colander and press gently with your fist to remove excess moisture.
2. Put the well-drained tomatoes into a bowl. Tear two of the basil leaves into small pieces and mix into the tomatoes. Set aside for a few minutes to allow the tomatoes to absorb the flavour of the basil.
3. Roll out the dough into a circle with a slightly thicker edge (*cornicione*). Spread the tomatoes evenly over the dough, but leave the edge (about 2cm/¾in) without tomato. Season wih salt and sprinkle olive oil over the pizza. Arrange the slices of mozzarella or *fior di latte* in the middle of the pizza. Bake in the centre of the oven. Garnish the pizza with the rest of the basil leaves before serving.

Calzone

In Naples, this is known quite simply as filled pizza.

RECIPE FOR A PIZZA FOR ONE PERSON.

START WITH THE DOUGH ON PAGE 122. DIVIDE THE DOUGH INTO FOUR AND USE ONE PIECE FOR EACH PERSON
OVEN TEMPERATURE: 275°C (525°F) – SEE PAGE 121
BAKING TIME: ABOUT 10–12 MINUTES – SEE PAGE 121

200G (7OZ) TOMATOES OF ONE OF THE FOLLOWING SORT:
CHERRY TOMATOES, CUT INTO HALVES
SAN MARZANO TOMATOES OR SIMILAR ITALIAN PLUM TOMATOES, CUT LENGTHWISE INTO 5MM (¼IN) SLICES
WHOLE CANNED TOMATOES, CRUSHED BY HAND AND DRAINED

100G (3½OZ) MOZZARELLA (THE ORIGINAL MADE FROM BUFFALO MILK) OR *FIOR DI LATTE*
(MOZZARELLA MADE FROM COW'S MILK), CUT INTO 1 X 1CM (½IN) CUBES
5–6 FRESH BASIL LEAVES
SALT
ABOUT 1 TBSP EXTRA-VIRGIN OLIVE OIL, PREFERABLY ITALIAN

1. Always let the tomatoes drain thoroughly before use to prevent the pizza becoming soggy. Drain canned tomatoes in a colander. Fresh tomatoes need some help. Put the sliced tomatoes into a colander and press them gently with your fist to remove as much moisture as possible. The same applies to mozzarella made from buffalo milk. Put the mozzarella slices into a colander and press gently with your fist to remove excess moisture.
2. Put the well-drained tomatoes into a bowl. Tear the basil leaves into small pieces and mix into the tomatoes. Set aside for a few minutes to allow the tomatoes to absorb the flavour of the basil.
3. Roll out the dough into a circle with a slightly thicker edge *(cornicione)*. Spread the tomatoes and basil over one half of the dough, but leave the edge (about 2cm/¾in) without tomato. Season with salt and spread the cubes of mozzarella or *fior di latte* over the tomatoes. Fold the uncovered half of the dough over the filling. Pinch the edges firmly together so that none of the moisture can escape. Bake in the centre of the oven until the top half of the dough has risen. Brush the pizza with a little olive oil before serving.

Pizza Canzone del Mare

The Song of the Sea is the name of a restaurant in Capri where I tasted sweet, sun-ripened cherry tomatoes for the first time. Only those kind of tomatoes are good enough for this pizza.

RECIPE FOR A PIZZA FOR ONE PERSON.

START WITH THE DOUGH ON PAGE 122. DIVIDE THE DOUGH INTO FOUR AND USE ONE PIECE FOR EACH PERSON
OVEN TEMPERATURE: 275°C (525°F) – SEE PAGE 121
BAKING TIME: ABOUT 10-12 MINUTES – SEE PAGE 121

200G (7OZ) CHERRY TOMATOES, CUT INTO HALVES
TWO EXTRA SMALL SPRIGS OF WHOLE CHERRY TOMATOES
6-8 FRESH BASIL LEAVES
3 CLOVES GARLIC, THICKLY SLICED
SALT
ABOUT 1 TBSP EXTRA-VIRGIN OLIVE OIL, PREFERABLY ITALIAN

1. Always let the tomatoes drain thoroughly before use to prevent the pizza becoming soggy. Put the sliced tomatoes into a colander and press them gently with your fist to remove as much moisture as possible.
2. Put the sliced, well-drained tomatoes into a bowl. Tear half the basil leaves into small pieces and mix into the tomatoes. Set aside for a few minutes to allow the tomatoes to absorb the flavour of the basil.
3. Roll out the dough into a circle with a slightly thicker edge (*cornicione*). Spread the sliced tomato and torn basil evenly over the dough, together with the extra sprigs of tomatoes and the garlic, but leave the edge (about 2cm/¾in) without tomato. Season with salt and sprinkle olive oil over the pizza. Bake in the centre of the oven. Garnish the pizza with the rest of the basil before serving.

Pizza Sant'Agata

Pizza with tomatoes, basil and smoked cheese. I got the inspiration for this pizza from Don Alfonso in the village of Sant'Agata sui due Golfi on the Sorrento peninsula. I was served *gnocchetti di patate* (fresh potato pasta) with cherry tomatoes from Vesuvius, fresh basil and melted *scamorza affumicata* (smoked cheese from Naples). It was so delicious that I returned the next evening for another serving. If you can find ripe, sweet cherry tomatoes, they are the best for this pizza.

RECIPE FOR A PIZZA FOR ONE PERSON.

START WITH THE DOUGH ON PAGE 122. DIVIDE THE DOUGH INTO FOUR AND USE ONE PIECE FOR EACH PERSON
OVEN TEMPERATURE: 275°C (525°F) – SEE PAGE 121
BAKING TIME: ABOUT 10–12 MINUTES – SEE PAGE 121

200G (7OZ) TOMATOES OF ONE OF THE FOLLOWING SORT:
CHERRY TOMATOES, CUT INTO HALVES
SAN MARZANO TOMATOES OR SIMILAR ITALIAN PLUM TOMATOES, CUT LENGTHWISE INTO 5MM (¼IN) SLICES
WHOLE CANNED TOMATOES, CRUSHED BY HAND AND DRAINED

5–6 FRESH BASIL LEAVES
SALT
ABOUT 1 TBSP EXTRA-VIRGIN OLIVE OIL, PREFERABLY ITALIAN
75G (2¾OZ) *SCAMORZA AFFUMICATA* OR OTHER SEMI-FAT SMOKED CHEEESE, SLICED

1. Always let the tomatoes drain thoroughly before use to prevent the pizza from becoming soggy. Drain canned tomatoes in a colander. Fresh tomatoes need some help. Put the sliced tomatoes into a colander and press them gently with your fist to remove as much moisture as possible.
2. Put the well-drained tomatoes into a bowl. Tear two of the basil leaves into small pieces and mix in with the tomatoes. Set aside for a few minutes to allow the tomatoes to absorb the flavour of the basil.
3. Roll out out the dough into a circle with a slightly thicker edge (*cornicione*). Spread the tomatoes evenly over the dough, but leave the edge (about 2cm/¾in) without tomato. Season with salt and sprinkle olive oil over the pizza. Put the slices of smoked cheese in the middle of the pizza. Bake in the centre of the oven. Garnish with the rest of the basil leaves before serving.

Pizza alle acciughe

Pizza with anchovies.

RECIPE FOR A PIZZA FOR ONE PERSON.

START WITH THE DOUGH ON PAGE 122. DIVIDE THE DOUGH INTO FOUR AND USE ONE PIECE FOR EACH PERSON
OVEN TEMPERATURE: 275°C (525°F) – PAGE 121
BAKING TIME: ABOUT 10-12 MINUTES – PAGE 121

200G (7OZ) TOMATOES OF ONE OF THE FOLLOWING SORT:
CHERRY TOMATOES, CUT INTO HALVES
SAN MARZANO TOMATOES OR SIMILAR ITALIAN PLUM TOMATOES, CUT LENGTHWISE INTO 5MM (¼IN) SLICES
WHOLE CANNED TOMATOES, CRUSHED BY HAND AND DRAINED

50G (1¾OZ) MOZZARELLA (THE ORIGINAL MADE FROM BUFFALO MILK) OR *FIOR DI LATTE* (MOZZARELLA MADE FROM COW'S MILK), SLICED
5 ANCHOVY FILLETS, CANNED IN OLIVE OIL, DRAINED (OIL PREFERABLY RESERVED) AND CUT INTO PIECES
2-3 SPRIGS OF FRESH THYME OR ½ TSP DRIED
SALT AND FRESHLY GROUND PEPPER
ABOUT 1 TBSP EXTRA-VIRGIN OLIVE OIL, PREFERABLY ITALIAN (IF NOT USING THE OLIVE OIL FROM THE CANNED ANCHOVIES)

1. Always let the tomatoes drain thoroughly before use to prevent the pizza from becoming soggy.
Drain canned tomatoes in a colander. Fresh tomatoes need some help. Put the sliced tomatoes into
a colander and press them gently with your fist to remove as much moisture as possible. The same applies
to mozzarella made from buffalo milk. Put the mozzarella slices into a colander and press gently with
your fist to remove excess moisture.
2. Roll out the dough into a circle with a slightly thicker edge (*cornicione*). Spread the tomatoes evenly over
the dough, but leave the edge (about 2cm/¾in) without tomato. Spread the pieces of anchovy and sprinkle half
the thyme over the tomatoes. Season sparingly with salt and grind over pepper. Sprinkle the pizza with olive
oil, preferably using that from the anchovy can. Arrange the slices of mozzarella or *fior di latte* in the middle
of the pizza. Bake in the centre of the oven. Garnish the pizza with the rest of the thyme before serving.

Pizza capperi, olive e acciughe

Pizza capperi, olive e acciughe

Pizza with capers, olives and anchovies. One of my absolute favourite pizzas, a real Neapolitan macho pizza. Excellently suited to the shade on a hot summer's day, preferably with a glass of chilled white wine.

RECIPE FOR A PIZZA FOR ONE PERSON.

START WITH THE DOUGH ON PAGE 122. DIVIDE THE DOUGH INTO FOUR AND USE ONE PIECE FOR EACH PERSON
OVEN TEMPERATURE: 275°C (525°F) – PAGE 121
BAKING TIME: ABOUT 10–12 MINUTES – PAGE 121

200G (7OZ) TOMATOES OF ONE OF THE FOLLOWING SORT:
CHERRY TOMATOES, CUT INTO HALVES
SAN MARZANO TOMATOES OR SIMILAR ITALIAN PLUM TOMATOES, CUT LENGTHWISE INTO 5MM (¼IN) SLICES
WHOLE CANNED TOMATOES, CRUSHED BY HAND AND DRAINED

10 ANCHOVY FILLETS, CANNED IN OLIVE OIL, DRAINED (OIL PREFERABLY RESERVED)
ABOUT 2 TBSP CAPERS
ABOUT 5 OLIVES, PITTED AND CUT INTO PIECES
1 TSP DRIED OREGANO
ABOUT 1 TBSP EXTRA-VIRGIN OLIVE OIL, PREFERABLY ITALIAN (IF NOT USING THE OLIVE OIL FROM THE CANNED ANCHOVIES)

1. Always let the tomatoes drain thoroughly before use to prevent the pizza from becoming soggy. Drain canned tomatoes in a colander. Fresh tomatoes need some help. Put the sliced tomatoes into a colander and press them gently with your fist to remove as much moisture as possible.
2. Roll out out the dough into a circle with a slightly thicker edge (*cornicione*). Spread the tomatoes evenly over the dough, but leave the edge (about 2cm/¾in) without tomato. Arrange the whole anchovy fillets on the pizza, then the capers and the olives. Sprinkle the pizza with oregano and olive oil, preferably using that from the anchovy can. This pizza needs no extra salt. Bake in the centre of the oven.

Pizza al tonno

Pizza with tuna fish.

RECIPE FOR A PIZZA FOR ONE PERSON.

START WITH THE DOUGH ON PAGE 122. DIVIDE THE DOUGH INTO FOUR AND USE ONE PIECE FOR EACH PERSON
OVEN TEMPERATURE: 275°C (525°F) – SEE PAGE 121
BAKING TIME: ABOUT 10–12 MINUTES – SEE PAGE 121

200G (7OZ) TOMATOES OF ONE OF THE FOLLOWING SORT:
CHERRY TOMATOES, CUT INTO HALVES
SAN MARZANO TOMATOES OR SIMILAR ITALIAN PLUM TOMATOES, CUT LENGTHWISE INTO 5MM (¼IN) SLICES
WHOLE CANNED TOMATOES, CRUSHED BY HAND AND DRAINED

100G (3½OZ) TUNA FISH, CANNED IN OLIVE OIL (USE THE VARIETY CANNED AS A WHOLE STEAK)
2 CLOVES GARLIC, THICKLY SLICED
ABOUT 2 TBSP CAPERS
1 FRESH RED CHILLI PEPPER *(PEPERONCINO FORTE)*, THINLY SLICED, OR ½ TSP DRIED AND GROUND
TWO SPRIGS OF FRESH MARJORAM OR THYME OR ½ TSP DRIED, PREFERABLY THYME
SALT AND FRESHLY GROUND PEPPER
ABOUT 1 TBSP EXTRA-VIRGIN OLIVE OIL, PREFERABLY ITALIAN

1. Always let the tomatoes drain thoroughly before use to prevent the pizza from becoming soggy. Drain canned tomatoes in a colander. Fresh tomatoes need some help. Put the sliced tomatoes into a colander and press them gently with your fist to remove as much moisture as possible.
2. Roll out the dough into a circle with a slightly thicker edge *(cornicione)*. Spread the tomatoes evenly over the dough, but leave the edge (about 2cm/¾in) without tomato. Spread the tuna fish, sliced garlic, capers, *peperoncino* and half the herbs over the tomatoes. Season with salt and pepper, and sprinkle the pizza with olive oil. Bake in the centre of the oven. Garnish the pizza with the rest of the herbs before serving.

Pizza alle vongole

Pizza with clams.

START WITH THE DOUGH ON PAGE 122. DIVIDE THE DOUGH INTO FOUR AND USE ONE PIECE FOR EACH PERSON
OVEN TEMPERATURE: 275°C (525°F) – SEE PAGE 121
BAKING TIME: ABOUT 10–12 MINUTES – SEE PAGE 121

200G (7OZ) TOMATOES OF ONE OF THE FOLLOWING SORT:
CHERRY TOMATOES, CUT INTO HALVES
SAN MARZANO TOMATOES OR SIMILAR ITALIAN PLUM TOMATOES, CUT LENGTHWISE INTO 5MM (¼IN) SLICES
WHOLE CANNED TOMATOES, CRUSHED BY HAND AND DRAINED

200G (7OZ) CLAMS (OR MUSSELS – PREPARATION IS THE SAME), IN THEIR SHELLS
200ML (7FL OZ) WATER, FOR COOKING THE CLAMS
A GOOD HANDFUL OF CHOPPED FRESH FLAT LEAF PARSLEY
1 CLOVE GARLIC, FINELY CHOPPED
SALT AND FRESHLY GROUND PEPPER
ABOUT 1 TBSP EXTRA-VIRGIN OLIVE OIL, PREFERABLY ITALIAN

1. Always let the tomatoes drain thoroughly before use to prevent the pizza from becoming soggy. Drain canned tomatoes in a colander. Fresh tomatoes need some help. Put the sliced tomatoes into a colander and press them gently with your fist to remove as much moisture as possible.

2. Rinse the clams carefully under running water to remove any sand. Remove any clams with broken shells and check that all the clams are closed. Tap any clams that are not closed gently on the sink; if they close up, they can be used. (If you use mussels, they should be scraped clean and any beards removed whilst rinsing.)

3. Quickly boil up the clams in the water, with a pinch of salt, for 1–2 minutes. Throw away any clams that do not open. Drain the clams in a sieve. The reason for cooking the clams before they are put in the oven is to remove as much moisture as possible. Shell half of the clams and discard the shells, saving the other half intact for putting on the pizza.

4. Roll out the dough into a circle with a slightly thicker edge (cornicione). Spread the tomatoes evenly over the dough, but leave the edge (about 2cm/¾in) without tomato. Sprinkle half the parsley over the tomatoes and scatter over the shelled clams and the chopped garlic. Then spread out the remaining clams with shells and the rest of the parsley. Season with salt and pepper and sprinkle the pizza with olive oil. Bake in the centre of the oven.

Pizza frutti di mare

Pizza with the fruits of the sea. This pizza requires quite a lot
of preparation, but the result is definitely worth it.

RECIPE FOR A PIZZA FOR ONE PERSON.

START WITH THE DOUGH ON PAGE 122. DIVIDE THE DOUGH INTO FOUR AND USE ONE PIECE FOR EACH PERSON
OVEN TEMPERATURE: 275°C (525°F) – SEE PAGE 121
BAKING TIME: 12 MINUTES – SEE PAGE 121

200G (7OZ) TOMATOES OF ONE OF THE FOLLOWING SORT:
CHERRY TOMATOES, CUT INTO HALVES
SAN MARZANO TOMATOES OR SIMILAR ITALIAN PLUM TOMATOES, CUT LENGTHWISE INTO 5MM (¼IN) SLICES
WHOLE CANNED TOMATOES, CRUSHED BY HAND AND DRAINED

100G (3½OZ) CLAMS, IN THEIR SHELLS
100G (3½OZ) MUSSELS, IN THEIR SHELLS
50G (1¾OZ) SQUID, CUT INTO THIN STRIPS (OPTIONAL)
300ML (½ PINT) WATER, FOR COOKING
½ TSP DRIED, GROUND CHILLI PEPPER (PEPERONCINO FORTE)
1 CLOVE GARLIC, FINELY CHOPPED
A GOOD HANDFUL OF CHOPPED FRESH FLAT LEAF PARSLEY
50G (1¾OZ) PEELED COOKED PRAWNS, PREFERABLY WITH THE SHELL LEFT ON THE TAILS IF YOU WISH TO EAT ALLA NAPOLETANA – WITH YOUR HANDS
2–3 UNPEELED COOKED PRAWNS
SALT AND FRESHLY GROUND PEPPER
ABOUT 1 TBSP EXTRA-VIRGIN OLIVE OIL, PREFERABLY ITALIAN

1. Always let the tomatoes drain thoroughly before use to prevent the pizza from becoming soggy. Drain canned tomatoes in a colander. Fresh tomatoes need some help. Put the sliced tomatoes into a colander and press them gently with your fist to remove as much moisture as possible.
2. Rinse the clams and mussels carefully under running water to remove any sand. Remove any clams or mussels with broken shells and check that they are all closed. Tap any clams or mussels that are not closed gently on the sink; if they close up, they can be used. Scrape the shells of the mussels clean with a small knife and remove any beards.
3. Quickly boil up the clams, mussels and squid (if using) in the water, with a pinch of salt, for 1–2 minutes. Throw away any clams and mussels that do not open. Drain the shellfish in a sieve. The reason for cooking the clams, mussels and squid before they are put in the oven is to remove as much moisture as possible.
4. Roll out the dough into a circle with a slightly thicker edge (cornicione). Spread the tomatoes evenly over the dough, but leave the edge (about 2cm/¾in) without tomato. Sprinkle the peperoncino, chopped garlic and half the parsley over the tomatoes. Then spread out the well-drained clams, mussels, squid and the peeled and unpeeled prawns. Sprinkle over the rest of the parsley. Season with salt and pepper and sprinkle the pizza with olive oil. Bake in the centre of the oven.

Pizza Verde

Green pizza.

RECIPE FOR A PIZZA FOR ONE PERSON.

START WITH THE DOUGH ON PAGE 122. DIVIDE THE DOUGH INTO FOUR AND USE ONE PIECE FOR EACH PERSON
OVEN TEMPERATURE: 275°C (525°F) – SEE PAGE 121
BAKING TIME: ABOUT 10–12 MINUTES – SEE PAGE 121

50G (1¾OZ) MOZZARELLA (THE ORIGINAL MADE FROM BUFFALO MILK) OR *FIOR DI LATTE* (MOZZARELLA MADE FROM COW'S MILK), SLICED
5 ANCHOVY FILLETS, CANNED IN OLIVE OIL, DRAINED
A HANDFUL OF FINELY CHOPPED FRESH FLAT LEAF PARSLEY
1 TBSP CHOPPED CAPERS
2 CLOVES GARLIC, FINELY CHOPPED
SALT AND FRESHLY GROUND PEPPER
ABOUT 2 TBSP EXTRA-VIRGIN OLIVE OIL, PREFERABLY ITALIAN
ABOUT 10 ROCKET LEAVES

1. Always let the mozzarella made from buffalo milk drain properly before use to prevent the pizza becoming soggy. Put the mozzarella slices into a colander and press gently with your fist to remove excess moisture.
2. Roll out the dough into a circle with a slightly thicker edge *(cornicione)*. Put the mozzarella or *fior di latte* on the dough (it won't cover the whole dough), but leave the edge (about 2cm/¾in) without. Spread the rest of the ingredients, except the rocket, over the cheese and the dough. Season with salt and pepper and sprinkle the pizza generously with olive oil. Bake in the centre of the oven. Garnish the pizza with the rocket before serving.

Pizza con gamberi e rucola

Pizza with prawns and rocket.

RECIPE FOR A PIZZA FOR ONE PERSON.

START WITH THE DOUGH ON PAGE 122. DIVIDE THE DOUGH INTO FOUR AND USE ONE PIECE FOR EACH PERSON
OVEN TEMPERATURE: 275°C (525°F) – SEE PAGE 121
BAKING TIME: ABOUT 10–12 MINUTES – SEE PAGE 121

200G (7OZ) TOMATOES OF ONE OF THE FOLLOWING SORT:
CHERRY TOMATOES, CUT INTO HALVES
SAN MARZANO TOMATOES OR SIMILAR ITALIAN PLUM TOMATOES, CUT LENGTHWISE INTO 5MM (¼IN) SLICES
WHOLE CANNED TOMATOES, CRUSHED BY HAND AND DRAINED

1 CLOVE GARLIC, FINELY CHOPPED
8–10 PEELED COOKED PRAWNS, PREFERABLY WITH THE SHELL LEFT ON THE TAILS IF YOU WISH TO EAT *ALLA NAPOLETANA* – WITH YOUR HANDS
ABOUT 10 BLACK OLIVES, WITH STONES
½ TSP FENNEL SEEDS
SALT AND FRESHLY GROUND PEPPER
ABOUT 1 TBSP EXTRA-VIRGIN OLIVE OIL, PREFERABLY ITALIAN
ABOUT 10 ROCKET LEAVES

1. Always let the tomatoes drain thoroughly before use to prevent the pizza from becoming soggy. Drain canned tomatoes in a colander. Fresh tomatoes need some help. Put the sliced tomatoes into a colander and press them gently with your fist to remove as much moisture as possible.
2. Roll out the dough into a circle with a slightly thicker edge (*cornicione*). Spread the tomatoes evenly over the dough, but leave the edge (about 2cm/¾in) without tomato. Spread the garlic over the tomatoes. Scatter over the prawns and the olives. Sprinkle the fennel seeds over the pizza. Season with salt and pepper and sprinkle with olive oil. Bake in the centre of the oven. Garnish the pizza with the rocket before serving.

Pizza alla melanzana

Pizza with aubergine.

RECIPE FOR A PIZZA FOR ONE PERSON.

START WITH THE DOUGH ON PAGE 122. DIVIDE THE DOUGH INTO FOUR AND USE ONE PIECE FOR EACH PERSON
OVEN TEMPERATURE: 275°C (525°F) – SEE PAGE 121
BAKING TIME: ABOUT 10–12 MINUTES – SEE PAGE 121

200G (7OZ) TOMATOES OF ONE OF THE FOLLOWING SORT:
CHERRY TOMATOES, CUT INTO HALVES
SAN MARZANO TOMATOES OR SIMILAR ITALIAN PLUM TOMATOES, CUT LENGTHWISE INTO 5MM (¼IN) SLICES
WHOLE CANNED TOMATOES, CRUSHED BY HAND AND DRAINED

50G (1¾OZ) MOZZARELLA (THE ORIGINAL MADE FROM BUFFALO MILK) OR *FIOR DI LATTE* (MOZZARELLA MADE FROM COW'S MILK), SLICED
100G (3½OZ) AUBERGINE, CUT INTO 1 X 1CM (¼IN) CUBES
ABOUT 2 TBSP EXTRA-VIRGIN OLIVE OIL, PREFERABLY ITALIAN
2 TBSP CAPERS
½ TSP DRIED OREGANO
1 CLOVE GARLIC, FINELY CHOPPED
SALT

1. Always let the tomatoes drain thoroughly before use to prevent the pizza from becoming soggy. Drain canned tomatoes in a colander. Fresh tomatoes need some help. Put the sliced tomatoes into a colander and press them gently with your fist to remove as much moisture as possible. The same applies to mozzarella made from buffalo milk. Put the mozzarella slices into a colander and press gently with your fist to remove excess moisture.
2. Fry the aubergine cubes in a hot, nonstick frying pan with very little olive oil until they are crisp on all sides. Add the well-drained tomatoes, capers, oregano and garlic to the frying pan. Mix together so that the aubergine cubes are covered in tomato.
3. Roll out the dough into a circle with a slightly thicker edge *(cornicione)*. Spread the tomato and aubergine mixture evenly over the dough, but leave the edge (about 2cm/¾in) without tomato. Season with salt and sprinkle the pizza with the rest of the olive oil. Arrange the slices of mozzarella or *fior di latte* in the middle of the pizza. Bake in the centre of the oven.

Pizza alle verdure

Pizza with vegetables. You will find most of the typical Neapolitan vegetables and flavours on this pizza.

RECIPE FOR A PIZZA FOR ONE PERSON.

START WITH THE DOUGH ON PAGE 122. DIVIDE THE DOUGH INTO FOUR AND USE ONE PIECE FOR EACH PERSON
OVEN TEMPERATURE: 275°C (525°F) – SEE PAGE 121
BAKING TIME: ABOUT 10–12 MINUTES – SEE PAGE 121

200G (7OZ) TOMATOES OF ONE OF THE FOLLOWING SORT:
CHERRY TOMATOES, CUT INTO HALVES
SAN MARZANO TOMATOES OR SIMILAR ITALIAN PLUM TOMATOES, CUT LENGTHWISE INTO 5MM (¼IN) SLICES
WHOLE CANNED TOMATOES, CRUSHED BY HAND AND DRAINED

100G (3½OZ) DIFFERENT COLOURED PEPPERS, DESEEDED AND CORED, CUT INTO SEGMENTS AND PEELED
50G (1¾OZ) COURGETTES, CUT LENGTHWISE INTO 5MM (¼IN) SLICES
50G (1¾OZ) AUBERGINES, CUT INTO 1 X 1CM (½IN) CUBES
ABOUT 2 TBSP EXTRA-VIRGIN OLIVE OIL, PREFERABLY ITALIAN
1 CLOVE GARLIC, FINELY CHOPPED
1 TSP FENNEL SEEDS
1 TBSP FINELY SHREDDED ORANGE OR LEMON ZEST – USE ONLY THE OUTER PEEL, AVOIDING THE WHITE PITH
ABOUT 5 BLACK OLIVES, PITTED AND CUT INTO PIECES
1 TBSP CAPERS
SALT

1. Always let the tomatoes drain thoroughly before use to prevent the pizza from becoming soggy. Drain canned tomatoes in a colander. Fresh tomatoes need some help. Put the sliced tomatoes into a colander and press them gently with your fist to remove as much moisture as possible.
2. Heat the grill until hot. Grill the peppers and courgettes for about 5 minutes, turn over and grill the other side. They should be turning a little black. Meanwhile, fry the aubergine cubes in a hot, nonstick frying pan with just a little olive oil until they are crisp on all sides.
3. Roll out the dough into a circle with a slightly thicker edge (*cornicione*). Spread the tomatoes evenly over the dough, but leave the edge (about 2cm/¾in) without tomato. Spread the garlic over the tomatoes. Scatter the grilled and fried vegetables over the pizza. Sprinkle with the fennel seeds, citrus peel, olives and capers. Season with salt and sprinkle the pizza with the rest of the olive oil. Bake in the centre of the oven.

Pizza con carciofi

Pizza with artichokes.

RECIPE FOR A PIZZA FOR ONE PERSON.

START WITH THE DOUGH ON PAGE 122. DIVIDE THE DOUGH INTO FOUR AND USE ONE PIECE FOR EACH PERSON
OVEN TEMPERATURE: 275°C (525°F) – SEE PAGE 121
BAKING TIME: ABOUT 10-12 MINUTES – SEE PAGE 121

50G (1¾OZ) MOZZARELLA (THE ORIGINAL MADE FROM BUFFALO MILK) OR *FIOR DI LATTE* (MOZZARELLA MADE FROM COW'S MILK), SLICED
100G (3½OZ) ARTICHOKE HEARTS, CANNED IN OLIVE OIL, DRAINED AND DIVIDED INTO SEGMENTS
1 CLOVE GARLIC, FINELY CHOPPED
½ TSP DRIED, GROUND CHILLI PEPPER *(PEPERONCINO FORTE)*
5-6 BLACK OLIVES, WITH STONES
3 TBSP CHOPPED FRESH FLAT LEAF PARSLEY
SALT AND FRESHLY GROUND PEPPER
ABOUT 1 TBSP EXTRA-VIRGIN OLIVE OIL, PREFERABLY ITALIAN
A SPRIG OF CHERRY TOMATOES (OPTIONAL)

1. Always let mozzarella made from buffalo milk drain thoroughly before use to prevent the pizza from becoming soggy. Put the mozzarella slices into a colander and press gently with your fist to remove excess moisture.
2. Roll out the dough into a circle with a slightly thicker edge *(cornicione)*. Spread the segments of artichoke hearts evenly over the dough, but leave the edge (about 2cm/¾in) without. Spread the garlic, *peperoncino*, olives and half the chopped parsley over the artichokes. Season with salt and pepper and sprinkle with olive oil. Arrange the slices of mozzarella or *fior di latte* in the middle of the pizza with the sprig of cherry tomatoes (if using). Bake in the centre of the oven. Garnish the pizza with the rest of the parsley before serving.

Pizza con peperoncino dolce

Sweet, green chilli peppers, *peperoncino dolce*, can be found in Naples during the summer. These are fried and eaten whole, and they are also delicious grilled whole on a pizza. They taste very similar to green peppers, so if you can't find *peperoncino dolce*, green peppers will do.

RECIPE FOR A PIZZA FOR ONE PERSON.

START WITH THE DOUGH ON PAGE 122. DIVIDE THE DOUGH INTO FOUR AND USE ONE PIECE FOR EACH PERSON
OVEN TEMPERATURE: 275°C (525°F) – SEE PAGE 121
BAKING TIME: ABOUT 10–12 MINUTES – SEE PAGE 121

200G (7OZ) TOMATOES OF ONE OF THE FOLLOWING SORT:
CHERRY TOMATOES, CUT INTO HALVES
SAN MARZANO TOMATOES OR SIMILAR ITALIAN PLUM TOMATOES, CUT LENGTHWISE INTO 5MM (¼IN) SLICES
WHOLE CANNED TOMATOES, CRUSHED BY HAND AND DRAINED

50G (1¾OZ) MOZZARELLA (THE ORIGINAL MADE FROM BUFFALO MILK) OR *FIOR DI LATTE* (MOZZARELLA MADE FROM COW'S MILK), SLICED
75G (2¾OZ) WHOLE *PEPERONCINO DOLCE* OR SEGMENTS OF GREEN PEPPER
½ TSP FENNEL SEEDS
1 CLOVE GARLIC, FINELY CHOPPED
ABOUT 10 BLACK OLIVES, WITH STONES
SALT
ABOUT 1 TBSP EXTRA-VIRGIN OLIVE OIL, PREFERABLY ITALIAN

1. Always let the tomatoes drain thoroughly before use to prevent the pizza from becoming soggy. Drain canned tomatoes in a colander. Fresh tomatoes need some help. Put the sliced tomatoes into a colander and press them gently with your fist to remove as much moisture as possible. The same applies to mozzarella made from buffalo milk. Put the mozzarella slices into a colander and press gently with your fist to remove excess moisture.

2. Heat the grill until hot. Grill the whole *peperoncino*, or pepper segments with the skin upwards, for 5–8 minutes, turning the *peperoncino* (not the green pepper) once. The skin should be turning a little black.

3. Roll out the dough into a circle with a slightly thicker edge (*cornicione*). Spread the tomatoes evenly over the dough, but leave the edge (about 2cm/¾in) without tomato. Sprinkle with fennel seeds and garlic. Scatter over the *peperoncino* or green pepper and the olives. Season with salt and sprinkle the pizza with olive oil. Arrange the slices of mozzarella or *fior di latte* in the middle of the pizza. Bake in the centre of the oven.

Pizza con cipolle

Pizza with onion.

RECIPE FOR A PIZZA FOR ONE PERSON.

START WITH THE DOUGH ON PAGE 122. DIVIDE THE DOUGH INTO FOUR AND USE ONE PIECE FOR EACH PERSON
OVEN TEMPERATURE: 275°C (525°F) – SEE PAGE 121
BAKING TIME: ABOUT 10-2 MINUTES – SEE PAGE 121

50G (1¾OZ) MOZZARELLA (THE ORIGINAL MADE FROM BUFFALO MILK) OR *FIOR DI LATTE* (MOZZARELLA MADE FROM COW'S MILK), SLICED
½ MEDIUM-SIZED ONION, THINLY SLICED
ABOUT 1 TBSP EXTRA-VIRGIN OLIVE OIL, PREFERABLY ITALIAN
A SPRIG OF FRESH ROSEMARY OR ½ TSP DRIED
A SPRIG OF FRESH THYME OR ½ TSP DRIED
SALT
A SPRIG OF CHERRY TOMATOES (OPTIONAL)

1. Always let the mozzarella made from buffalo milk drain thoroughly before use to prevent the pizza from becoming soggy. Put the mozzarella slices into a colander and press gently with your fist to remove excess moisture.
2. Fry the onion quickly in a little olive oil until it is soft but not coloured.
3. Roll out the dough into a circle with a slightly thicker edge *(cornicione)*. Sprinkle the fried onion evenly over the dough, but leave the edge (about 2cm/¾in) without. Sprinkle over most of the herbs. Season with salt and sprinkle with rest of the olive oil. Arrange the slices of mozzarella or *fior di latte* in the centre of the pizza and place a sprig of cherry tomatoes (if using) in the middle of the mozzarella. Bake in the centre of the oven. Garnish with the rest of the herbs before serving.

Pizza ai broccoli

Pizza with broccoli. My father Enzo has taught me to appreciate lemon and orange peel as seasoning. They are widely used in southern Italian cuisine. My father's hot, garlic-pungent pepper casserole, *peperonata*, with orange peel is one of my favourite dishes. I use finely shredded lemon zest here to give extra flavour to my broccoli pizza.

RECIPE FOR A PIZZA FOR ONE PERSON.

START WITH THE DOUGH ON PAGE 122. DIVIDE THE DOUGH INTO FOUR AND USE ONE PIECE FOR EACH PERSON
OVEN TEMPERATURE: 275°C (525°F) – SEE PAGE 121
BAKING TIME: ABOUT 10–12 MINUTES – SEE PAGE 121

50G (1¾OZ) MOZZARELLA (THE ORIGINAL MADE FROM BUFFALO MILK) OR *FIOR DI LATTE* (MOZZARELLA MADE FROM COW'S MILK), SLICED
150G (5½OZ) BROCCOLI FLORETS, PARBOILED IF FRESH
1 TSP FENNEL SEEDS
1 CLOVE GARLIC, FINELY CHOPPED
1 FRESH RED CHILLI PEPPER *(PEPERONCINO FORTE)*, THINLY SLICED, OR ½ TSP DRIED AND GROUND
1 TBSP FINELY SHREDDED ORANGE OR LEMON ZEST – USE ONLY THE OUTER PEEL, AVOIDING THE WHITE PITH
SALT
ABOUT 1 TBSP EXTRA-VIRGIN OLIVE OIL, PREFERABLY ITALIAN

1. Always let the mozzarella made from buffalo milk drain thoroughly before use to prevent the pizza from becoming soggy. Put the mozzarella slices into a colander and press gently with your fist to remove excess moisture.
2. If you use fresh broccoli, parboil it quickly in a little lightly salted water. Frozen broccoli only needs to be thawed. Let the broccoli drain thoroughly in a colander. Press carefully with a wooden fork to remove any excess moisture without breaking the florets.
3. Roll out the dough into a circle with a slightly thicker edge *(cornicione)*. Spread the broccoli evenly over the dough, but leave the edge (about 2cm/¾in) without. Sprinkle the fennel seeds, garlic, *peperoncino* and finally the shredded orange or lemon zest over the broccoli. Season with salt and sprinkle with olive oil. Arrange the slices of mozzarella or *fior di latte* in the middle of the pizza. Bake in the centre of the oven.

Pizza aglio, olio e peperoncino

A pizza inspired by the simplest of all spaghetti dishes, with garlic, olive oil and hot chilli pepper.

RECIPE FOR A PIZZA FOR ONE PERSON.

START WITH THE DOUGH ON PAGE 122. DIVIDE THE DOUGH INTO FOUR AND USE ONE PIECE FOR EACH PERSON
OVEN TEMPERATURE: 275°C (525°F) – SEE PAGE 121
BAKING TIME: ABOUT 5 MINUTES – SEE PAGE 121

50G (1¾OZ) MOZZARELLA (THE ORIGINAL MADE FROM BUFFALO MILK) OR *FIOR DI LATTE* (MOZZARELLA MADE FROM COW'S MILK), SLICED
ABOUT 2–3 TBSP EXTRA-VIRGIN OLIVE OIL, PREFERABLY ITALIAN
1 CLOVE GARLIC, FINELY CHOPPED
1 FRESH RED CHILLI PEPPER *(PEPERONCINO FORTE)*, THINLY SLICED, OR ½ TSP DRIED AND GROUND
SALT
FRESHLY GROUND BLACK PEPPER OR WHOLE BLACK PEPPERCORNS, CRUSHED IN A MORTAR
A FEW LEAVES OF FRESH FLAT LEAF PARSLEY

1. Always let the mozzarella made from buffalo milk drain thoroughly before use to prevent the pizza from becoming soggy. Put the mozzarella slices into a colander and press gently with your fist to remove excess moisture.

2. Roll out the dough into a circle with a slightly thicker edge (*cornicione*). Sprinkle olive oil evenly over the dough, but leave the edge (about 2cm/¾in) without. Scatter the garlic and *peperoncino* over the oil and season with salt. Arrange the slices of mozzarella or *fior di latte* in the middle of the pizza. Grind or sprinkle a generous amount of black pepper over the pizza. Bake in the centre of the oven. Garnish with the parsley before serving.

154

Pizza Bianca

Who says pizzas have to be red? Pizzas without tomatoes are called white pizzas in Naples. This pizza really lives up to that name. The pizza is tastiest with mozzarella made from buffalo milk, since it has more flavour and is a little more fatty than *fior di latte*.

RECIPE FOR A PIZZA FOR ONE PERSON.

START WITH THE DOUGH ON PAGE 122. DIVIDE THE DOUGH INTO FOUR AND USE ONE PIECE FOR EACH PERSON
OVEN TEMPERATURE: 275°C (525°F) – SEE PAGE 121
BAKING TIME: ABOUT 6–8 MINUTES – SEE PAGE 121

100G (3½OZ) MOZZARELLA (THE ORIGINAL MADE FROM BUFFALO MILK) OR *FIOR DI LATTE* (MOZZARELLA MADE FROM COW'S MILK), SLICED
SALT
ABOUT 1 TBSP EXTRA-VIRGIN OLIVE OIL, PREFERABLY ITALIAN
FRESHLY GROUND BLACK PEPPER OR WHOLE BLACK PEPPERCORNS, CRUSHED IN A MORTAR

1. Always let the mozzarella made from buffalo milk drain thoroughly before use to prevent the pizza from becoming soggy. Put the mozzarella slices into a colander and press gently with your fist to remove excess moisture.
2. Roll out the dough into a circle with a slightly thicker edge *(cornicione)*. Spread the mozzarella or *fior di latte* evenly over the dough, but leave the edge (about 2cm/¾in) without. Season the pizza with salt and sprinkle with olive oil. Bake in the centre of the oven. Grind or sprinkle a generous amount of black pepper over the pizza before serving.

Pizza ai due formaggi

There are many ways to make white pizza. Here is a version with two different cheeses and fresh herbs.
I have used mozzarella and smoked cheese. You can use the cheese you like most, but the result is best
with mozzarella and a couple of slices of a strongly flavoured cheese.

RECIPE FOR A PIZZA FOR ONE PERSON.

START WITH THE DOUGH ON PAGE 122. DIVIDE THE DOUGH INTO FOUR AND USE ONE PIECE FOR EACH PERSON
OVEN TEMPERATURE: 275°C (525°F) – SEE PAGE 121
BAKING TIME: ABOUT 10–12 MINUTES – SEE PAGE 121

50G (1¾OZ) MOZZARELLA (THE ORIGINAL MADE FROM BUFFALO MILK) OR *FIOR DI LATTE* (MOZZARELLA MADE FROM COW'S MILK), SLICED
20G (¾OZ) *SCAMORZA AFFUMICATA* OR OTHER SMOKED OR STRONGLY FLAVOURED CHEESE
ABOUT 10 OLIVES, WITH STONES
A LITTLE SPRIG OF FRESH ROSEMARY OR 1 TSP DRIED
1-2 SAGE LEAVES OR OTHER FRESH HERB, SUCH AS THYME OR MARJORAM
SALT
ABOUT 1 TBSP EXTRA-VIRGIN OLIVE OIL, PREFERABLY ITALIAN

1. Always let the mozzarella made from buffalo milk drain thoroughly before use to prevent the pizza from
becoming soggy. Put the mozzarella slices into a colander and press gently with your fist to remove excess
moisture.
2. Roll out the dough into a circle with a slightly thicker edge (*cornicione*). Spread the mozzarella or *fior di latte*
evenly over the dough, but leave the edge (about 2cm/¾in) without. Arrange the *scamorza* in the middle of the
pizza. Scatter the olives and herbs over the cheese. Season with salt and sprinkle the pizza with olive oil. Bake
in the centre of the oven.

Pizza ai quattro formaggi

Pizza with four cheeses. This pizza is usually made with mozzarella and typical north Italian or north European varieties of cheese. I have made this version with Neapolitan cheeses, but you can use the cheeses you like best. The cheeses should be of a full-fat or semi-fat kind and have different flavours: sharp, mild or matured blue cheese varieties. One of them should, however, be mozzarella.

RECIPE FOR A PIZZA FOR ONE PERSON.

START WITH THE DOUGH ON PAGE 122. DIVIDE THE DOUGH INTO FOUR AND USE ONE PIECE FOR EACH PERSON
OVEN TEMPERATURE: 275°C (525°F) – SEE PAGE 121
BAKING TIME: ABOUT 10–12 MINUTES – SEE PAGE 121

20G (¾OZ) MOZZARELLA (THE ORIGINAL MADE FROM BUFFALO MILK) OR *FIOR DI LATTE* (MOZZARELLA MADE FROM COW'S MILK), SLICED
20G (¾OZ) *CACIO CAVALLO*, SLICED
20G (¾OZ) *PROVOLONE PICCANTE*, SLICED
20G (¾OZ) *SCAMORZA AFFUMICATA*, SLICED
A SPRIG OF FRESH ROSEMARY OR 1 TSP DRIED

1. Always let the mozzarella made from buffalo milk drain thoroughly before use to prevent the pizza from becoming soggy. Put the mozzarella slices into a colander and press gently with your fist to remove the excess moisture.
2. Roll out the dough into a circle with a slightly thicker edge (*cornicione*). Arrange the cheeses in groups evenly over the dough, but leave the edge (about 2cm/¾in) without. Scatter half the rosemary leaves over the pizza. Bake in the centre of the oven. Garnish with the rest of the rosemary before serving.

Pizza Bianca al rosmarino

White pizza with rosemary. My version is not completely white – a sprig of cherry tomatoes add a dash of red, but the pizza is nearly as good without.

RECIPE FOR A PIZZA FOR ONE PERSON.

START WITH THE DOUGH ON PAGE 122. DIVIDE THE DOUGH INTO FOUR AND USE ONE PIECE FOR EACH PERSON
OVEN TEMPERATURE: 275°C (525°F) – SEE PAGE 121
BAKING TIME: ABOUT 8–10 MINUTES – SEE PAGE 121

100G (3½OZ) MOZZARELLA (THE ORIGINAL MADE FROM BUFFALO MILK) OR *FIOR DI LATTE* (MOZZARELLA MADE FROM COW'S MILK), SLICED
A LITTLE SPRIG OF FRESH ROSEMARY OR 1 TSP DRIED
A SPRIG OF CHERRY TOMATOES
SALT
ABOUT 1 TBSP EXTRA-VIRGIN OLIVE OIL, PREFERABLY ITALIAN
3–4 FRESH SAGE LEAVES

1. Always let the mozzarella made from buffalo milk drain thoroughly before use to prevent the pizza from becoming soggy. Put the mozzarella slices into a colander and press gently with your fist to remove excess moisture.
2. Roll out the dough into a circle with a slightly thicker edge (*cornicione*). Spread the mozzarella or *fior di latte* evenly over the dough, but leave the edge (about 2cm/¾in) without. Scatter the rosemary leaves over the pizza and finish with a sprig of cherry tomatoes in the middle. Season with salt and sprinkle the pizza with olive oil. Bake in the centre of the oven. Scatter the sage leaves over the pizza before serving.

Pizza Il vecchietto

I am not really sure why this pizza is called the 'old man' – maybe because the ingredients seem as if they have always been around or because the sheep's cheese should be very mature.

RECIPE FOR A PIZZA FOR ONE PERSON.

START WITH THE DOUGH ON PAGE 122. DIVIDE THE DOUGH INTO FOUR AND USE ONE PIECE FOR EACH PERSON
OVEN TEMPERATURE: 275°C (525°F) – SEE PAGE 121
BAKING TIME: ABOUT 10–2 MINUTES – SEE PAGE 121

20G (¾OZ) MOZZARELLA (THE ORIGINAL MADE FROM BUFFALO MILK) OR *FIOR DI LATTE* (MOZZARELLA MADE FROM COW'S MILK), SLICED
50G (1¾OZ) *PECORINO STAGIONATO* (OR SOME OTHER VERY MATURE SHEEP OR GOAT'S CHEESE), THINLY SLICED
50G (1¾OZ) RICOTTA OR OTHER FRESH CHEESE
A SPRIG OF CHERRY TOMATOES
20G (¾OZ) SALTED PORK, THINLY SLICED (THIN RASHERS OF STREAKY BACON WILL DO JUST AS WELL)
2 FRESH BAY LEAVES OR 1 DRIED
SALT AND FRESHLY GROUND PEPPER
ABOUT 1 TBSP EXTRA-VIRGIN OLIVE OIL, PREFERABLY ITALIAN

1. Always let the mozzarella made from buffalo milk drain thoroughly before use to prevent the pizza from becoming soggy. Put the mozzarella slices into a colander and press gently with your fist to remove excess moisture.

2. Roll out the dough into a circle with a slightly thicker edge *(cornicione)*. Spread the pecorino over half the dough and the ricotta over a quarter (leave the other quarter empty), but leave the edge (about 2cm/¾in) without. Arrange the sprig of tomato over the pecorino, the mozzarella or the *fior di latte* over the ricotta and the pork or bacon over the empty part of the pizza. Put a bay leaf in the middle of the pizza. Season with salt and pepper and sprinkle with olive oil. Bake in the centre of the oven. If you are using fresh bay leaves, you should replace the one that has been in the oven with another fresh one; this is more decorative.

159

Pizza con caprino, pancetta e pomodoro fresco

Pizza con caprino, pancetta e pomodoro fresco

Pizza with fresh goat's cheese, salted pork and fresh tomatoes. *Caprino* is a typical southern Italian fresh cheese made from goat's milk. The tomatoes should be fresh. I have used thin slices of San Marzano tomatoes, but cherry tomatoes or another kind of tomato are just as good, provided they are red and firm.

RECIPE FOR A PIZZA FOR ONE PERSON.

START WITH THE DOUGH ON PAGE 122. DIVIDE THE DOUGH INTO FOUR AND USE ONE PIECE FOR EACH PERSON
OVEN TEMPERATURE: 275°C (525°F) – SEE PAGE 121
BAKING TIME: ABOUT 10–12 MINUTES – SEE PAGE 121

200G (7OZ) TOMATOES OF ONE OF THE FOLLOWING SORT:
CHERRY TOMATOES, CUT INTO HALVES
SAN MARZANO TOMATOES OR SIMILAR ITALIAN PLUM TOMATOES, CUT LENGTHWISE INTO 5MM (¼IN) SLICES
75G (2¾OZ) *CAPRINO* OR OTHER TYPE OF FRESH GOAT'S CHEESE, CRUMBLED
20G (¾OZ) SALTED PORK, THINLY SLICED (THIN RASHERS OF STREAKY BACON WILL DO JUST AS WELL)
A FEW SPRIGS OF FRESH THYME OR 1 TSP DRIED
SALT
ABOUT 1 TBSP EXTRA-VIRGIN OLIVE OIL, PREFERABLY ITALIAN

1. Always let the tomatoes drain thoroughly before use to prevent the pizza from becoming soggy. Put the sliced tomatoes into a colander and press them gently with your fist to remove as much moisture as possible.
2. Roll out the dough into a circle with a slightly thicker edge (*cornicione*). Spread the tomato, cheese and pork or bacon evenly over the dough, but leave the edge (about 2cm/¾in) without. Sprinkle half the thyme over the pizza. Season with salt and sprinkle the pizza with olive oil. Bake in the centre of the oven. Sprinkle the rest of the thyme over the pizza before serving.

Pizza con spinaci, ricotta e pancetta

Pizza with spinach, fresh cheese and salted pork.

RECIPE FOR A PIZZA FOR ONE PERSON.

START WITH THE DOUGH ON PAGE 122. DIVIDE THE DOUGH INTO FOUR AND USE ONE PIECE FOR EACH PERSON
OVEN TEMPERATURE: 275°C (525°F) – SEE PAGE 121
BAKING TIME: ABOUT 10–12 MINUTES – SEE PAGE 121

50G (1¾OZ) MOZZARELLA (THE ORIGINAL MADE FROM BUFFALO MILK) OR *FIOR DI LATTE* (MOZZARELLA MADE FROM COW'S MILK), SLICED
100G (3½OZ) SPINACH, PARBOILED
1 SMALL CLOVE GARLIC, FINELY CHOPPED
FRESHLY GRATED NUTMEG
100G (3½OZ) RICOTTA OR OTHER FRESH CHEESE
SALT
20G (¾OZ) SALTED PORK, THINLY SLICED (THIN RASHERS OF STREAKY BACON WILL DO JUST AS WELL)

1. Always let the mozzarella made from buffalo milk drain thoroughly before use to prevent the pizza from becoming soggy. Put the mozzarella slices into a colander and press gently with your fist to remove excess moisture.
2. If you are using fresh spinach, this should always be well rinsed and cleaned. Boil quickly in a cup (100ml/3½fl oz) of water. Put the spinach in a colander and press out as much moisture as possible.
3. Roll out the dough into a circle with a slightly thicker edge (*cornicione*). Spread the spinach and garlic evenly over the pizza. Grate a little nutmeg over the pizza. Arrange the slices of mozzarella or *fior di latte* in the middle of the pizza. Dot the ricotta over the pizza, season with salt and finally add the pork or bacon. Bake in the centre of the oven.

Pizza con salsiccia piccante

Pizza with spicy sausage.

RECIPE FOR A PIZZA FOR ONE PERSON.

START WITH THE DOUGH ON PAGE 122. DIVIDE THE DOUGH INTO FOUR AND USE ONE PIECE FOR EACH PERSON
OVEN TEMPERATURE: 275°C (525°F) – SEE PAGE 121
BAKING TIME: ABOUT 10–12 MINUTES – SEE PAGE 121

200G (7OZ) TOMATOES OF ONE OF THE FOLLOWING SORT:
CHERRY TOMATOES, CUT INTO HALVES
SAN MARZANO TOMATOES OR SIMILAR ITALIAN PLUM TOMATOES, CUT LENGTHWISE INTO 5MM (¼IN) SLICES
WHOLE CANNED TOMATOES, CRUSHED BY HAND AND DRAINED

50G (1¾OZ) MOZZARELLA (THE ORIGINAL MADE FROM BUFFALO MILK) OR *FIOR DI LATTE* (MOZZARELLA MADE FROM COW'S MILK), SLICED
100G (3½OZ) *SALSICCIA PICCANTE DI NAPOLI* OR A SIMILAR SPICY, ROUGHLY MINCED AND MATURED SALAMI-STYLE SAUSAGE, SLICED
1–2 SPRIGS FRESH THYME OR ½ TSP DRIED
SALT
ABOUT 1 TBSP EXTRA-VIRGIN OLIVE OIL, PREFERABLY ITALIAN
3–4 FRESH BASIL LEAVES

1. Always let the tomatoes drain thoroughly before use to prevent the pizza becoming soggy. Drain canned tomatoes in a colander. Fresh tomatoes need some help. Put the sliced tomatoes into a colander and press them gently with your fist to remove as much moisture as possible. The same applies to mozzarella made from buffalo milk. Put the mozzarella slices into a colander and press gently with your fist to remove excess moisture.
2. Roll out the dough into a circle with a slightly thicker edge *(cornicione)*. Spread the tomatoes evenly over the dough, but leave the edge (about 2cm/¾in) without tomato. Arrange the slices of sausage and thyme over the tomatoes. Season with salt and sprinkle olive oil over the pizza. Arrange the slices of mozzarella or *fior di latte* in the middle of the pizza. Bake in the centre of the oven. Garnish the pizza with the basil leaves before serving.

Pizza Mamma Matilde

When my mother came to Hallstahammar in Sweden from Taranto in Puglia in southern Italy in the 1940s, her parsley-filled meatballs were a great success. First they were fried lightly in a frying pan and then cooked in an aromatic tomato sauce until ready. This pizza is a tribute to my mother's meatballs.

RECIPE FOR A PIZZA FOR ONE PERSON.

START WITH THE DOUGH ON PAGE 122. DIVIDE THE DOUGH INTO FOUR AND USE ONE PIECE FOR EACH PERSON
OVEN TEMPERATURE: 275°C (525°F) – SEE PAGE 121
BAKING TIME: ABOUT 10–12 MINUTES – SEE PAGE 121

200G (7OZ) TOMATOES OF ONE OF THE FOLLOWING SORT:
CHERRY TOMATOES, CUT INTO HALVES
SAN MARZANO TOMATOES OR SIMILAR ITALIAN PLUM TOMATOES, CUT LENGTHWISE INTO 5MM (¼IN) SLICES
WHOLE CANNED TOMATOES, CRUSHED BY HAND AND DRAINED

50G (1¾OZ) MOZZARELLA (THE ORIGINAL MADE FROM BUFFALO MILK) OR *FIOR DI LATTE* (MOZZARELLA MADE FROM COW'S MILK), SLICED
150G (5½OZ) MIXED MINCED MEAT
1 EGG YOLK
1 TBSP BREADCRUMBS
A PINCH OF FRESHLY GRATED NUTMEG
A HANDFUL OF CHOPPED FRESH FLAT LEAF PARSLEY
SALT
ABOUT 1 TBSP EXTRA-VIRGIN OLIVE OIL, PREFERABLY ITALIAN
A FEW FRESH BASIL LEAVES

1. Always let the tomatoes drain thoroughly before use to prevent the pizza becoming soggy. Drain canned tomatoes in a colander. Fresh tomatoes need some help. Put the sliced tomatoes into a colander and press them gently with your fist to remove as much moisture as possible. The same applies to mozzarella made from buffalo milk. Put the mozzarella slices into a colander and press gently with your fist to remove excess moisture.
2. Mix together the minced meat, egg yolk, breadcrumbs, nutmeg, parsley and a generous pinch of salt in a bowl.
3. Roll out the dough into a circle with a slightly thicker edge (*cornicione*). Spread the tomatoes and minced meat mixture evenly over the dough, but leave the edge (about 2cm/¾in) without. Season with salt and sprinkle olive oil over the pizza. Arrange the slices of mozzarella or *fior di latte* in the middle of the pizza. Bake in the centre of the oven. Garnish with a few basil leaves in the middle of the pizza before serving.

The authentic Neapolitan pizzeria guide

Da Michele
Via Cesare Sersale 1/3 Tel. 081-5539204
Only pizza. Closed on Sundays.
IT'S THE REAL THING. MINIMAL DECOR WITH MARBLE TABLES AND WHITE WALL TILES JUST LIKE IN THE OLD DAYS, AND AUTHENTIC NEAPOLITAN PIZZA, I.E. MARGHERITA OR MARINARA. ONLY OTHER POSSIBLE CHOICE – A DELICIOUS CALZONE FULL OF *FIOR DI LATTE*. ON SATURDAY EVENINGS, BE PREPARED TO QUEUE FOR OVER AN HOUR. TAKE YOUR NUMBER AND WAIT YOUR TURN. CHAT WITH OTHER PEOPLE IN THE QUEUE AND RELAX. THERE'S NO POINT IN BEING IN A HURRY IN NAPLES.

Di Matteo
Via Tribunali 94 Tel. 081-455262
Only pizza. Closed on Sundays.
A STROLL DOWN VIA DEI TRIBUNALI, THE THROBBING HEART OF OLD NAPLES, IS AN EXPERIENCE IN ITSELF. BUT IF YOU WANT THE WHOLE NEAPOLITAN DEAL, YOU MUST STOP OFF FOR LUNCH AT DI MATTEO, THE PIZZERIA WHERE BILL CLINTON ATE. IN CASE YOU'D FORGOTTEN, THERE ARE SEVERAL PHOTOS OF THE MEMORABLE OCCASION ON THE WALL TO REMIND YOU. IF YOU DON'T HAVE ENOUGH TIME TO SIT DOWN INSIDE, DON'T WORRY – WITH A LITTLE PUSH AND SHOVE YOU SHOULD GET TO THE STREET COUNTER WHERE YOU CAN BUY A PIZZA *A LIBRETTO*, AS THEY SAY IN NAPLES. THIS PIZZA, FOLDED OVER TWICE, IS SPECIALLY DESIGNED TO BE EATEN STANDING ON THE PAVEMENT. OR, IF YOU PREFER, YOU CAN HAVE DEEP-FRIED PIZZA AND OTHER WONDERS, ALL FRESHLY COOKED TO ORDER.

Sorbillo
Via Tribunali, 35 No telephone.
Only pizza. Closed on Sundays.
ANOTHER UNMISSABLE, HISTORIC PIZZERIA. IN VIA DEI TRIBUNALI SINCE 1934, THIS PIZZERIA IS ALSO KNOWN AS DONNA ESTERINA'S, AFTER THE OWNER WHO WAITS AT THE TABLES AND, WHEN NECESSARY, DIRECTS THE TRAFFIC. THE PLACE IS TINY – ONLY SIX MARBLE TABLES ARRANGED BETWEEN THE WOOD OVEN AND THE FLOUR-COVERED WORKTOP. THE HISTORY OF THE PIZZERIA IS INEXTRICABLY LINKED TO THE HISTORY OF THE SORBILLO FAMILY AND IS RECOUNTED BY THE NEWSPAPER CUTTINGS WHOSE GRANDIOSE HEADLINES CELEBRATE THE BIRTHS OF LUIGI SORBILLO'S 21 CHILDREN. THOSE WERE THE TIMES WHEN MUSSOLINI REWARDED LARGE FAMILIES, THEY TELL YOU. AND IN THE MEANTIME THEY BRING YOU A DELICIOUS MARGHERITA. TWO DOORS UP THE ROAD, AFTER THE BAKER'S AND THE WINE-SHOP, ANOTHER PIZZERIA SORBILLO HAS RECENTLY OPENED. NOT TO BE CONFUSED WITH THE REAL MCCOY. BUT THEN AGAIN, IT'S HARDLY SURPRISING. IN THIS ONE, THERE JUST ISN'T ENOUGH SPACE FOR 21 CHILDREN.

900
Via Pasquale Scura, 5 Tel. 081-5521634
Only pizza. Closed on Wednesdays.
ON THE VISITING CARD, IT SAYS *ONORATECI*: HONOUR US WITH YOUR PRESENCE. SO LET'S GO AHEAD AND HONOUR THIS SMALL PIZZERIA, WHICH IS NOT ESPECIALLY WELL-KNOWN AND HAS NO PHOTOS OF FAMOUS CLIENTS ON ITS WALLS. INSTEAD, THERE IS AN OVEN COVERED IN SMALL, RED TILES, SEA-GREEN WOODEN TABLES AND CHAIRS AND BRIGHT YELLOW PAPER TABLECLOTHS. EVERYTHING IS IN COLOUR IN THIS PLACE, INCLUDING THE SMALL TV BEHIND THE FLOUR-COVERED COUNTER, WHICH IS PERMANENTLY ON. THE PIZZAS ARE RICH AND TASTY. IF YOU'RE HUNGRY, WE RECOMMEND THE PIZZA 900 – *FIOR DI LATTE*, TOMATO, MUSHROOMS, HAM AND SAUSAGE. IF YOU'D RATHER HAVE A PIZZA WITH NO TOMATO, GO FOR PIZZA ALLA PARTENOPEA – *FIOR DI LATTE*, *FRIARELLI* (A KIND OF BROCCOLI) AND SAUSAGE. AND IF YOU THINK THE PIZZA IS GOOD, TELL THE PIZZA-MAKER, WHO'LL ANSWER: 'GOOD? NO, EXCEPTIONAL!'

7 Soldi
Vico Tre Re, 6 – angolo vico Lungo Gelso
Tel. 081-455262
Pizzeria and restaurant. Closed on Mondays.
NOT MANY PEOPLE HAVE COTTONED ON TO THE FACT THAT, IN THIS NARROW ALLEY BEHIND THE BUSY VIA TOLEDO, THERE IS A PIZZERIA THAT HASN'T CHANGED MUCH IN ITS 30 YEARS OF EXISTENCE, APART FROM THE RECENT ADDITION OF A SECOND DINING AREA. THE PLACE IS FREQUENTED BY LOCALS AND BY THE OCCASIONAL INTELLECTUAL OR ARTIST WHO DOESN'T WANT TO BE RECOGNIZED. ONE OF THE REASONS THEY COME HERE IS FOR THE PIZZA 7 SOLDI, THE HOUSE SPECIALITY THAT THE PIZZA-MAKER FRANCESCO LEARNED FROM HIS GRANDFATHER GENNARO – A PIZZA WITH SEVEN DIFFERENT INGREDIENTS ACCURATELY DIVIDED UP ON THE PIZZA BASE.

La Fila
Via Nazionale 6/B Tel. 081-206717
Pizzeria and restaurant. Closed on Mondays.
MEET DONNA ELVIRA AND YOU KNOW EVERYTHING THERE IS TO KNOW ABOUT HER PIZZERIA-RESTAURANT. OPENED BY HER HUSBAND GAETANO'S PARENTS ABOUT 15 YEARS AGO, IT'S JUST A FEW METRES FROM THE MAIN STATION. DONNA ELVIRA'S IRRESISTIBLE CHARACTER CREATES A WARM AND WELCOMING ATMOSPHERE. SHE TAKES ALL THE DECISIONS AROUND HERE, INCLUDING WHAT PIZZA TO BRING YOU. IF SHE DECIDES ON A FILA COMPLETA, YOU'RE IN FOR A TREAT. TOPPED WITH FRESH TOMATOES, MOZZARELLA, HAM AND MUSHROOMS, THE REAL SURPRISE IS IN THE BORDER, FILLED WITH RICOTTA. UNIQUE.

O' Calamaro
Viale Campi Flegrei 30 Tel. 081-5704387
Pizzeria and restaurant. Closed on Sundays.
THIS BUZZING PIZZERIA IS A LITTLE OFF THE BEATEN TRACK. BUT ITS CLIENTELE IS NOT JUST THE YOUTH FROM THE BAGNOLI AREA. MANY NEAPOLITANS MAKE THE EFFORT TO COME OUT HERE TO SAVOUR THE SPECIALITIES THAT HAVE MADE GENNARO ESPOSITO ONE OF THE BEST-KNOWN PIZZA-MAKERS IN TOWN, LIKE THE PIZZA CIGNO, SWAN PIZZA OR CONCHIGLIA, SHELL, WHICH WON FIRST PRIZE IN COUNTLESS PIZZA TOURNAMENTS!
A FEW SUGGESTIONS: THE BASTONE, FILLED WITH *PROVOLA, FRIARELLI* AND STRIPS OF TOMATO; THE BRACCIO DI FERRO PIZZA (*BRACCIO DI FERRO* IS POPEYE IN ITALIAN), WITH *FIOR DI LATTE*, SPINACH AND RICOTTA; AND, HIS LATEST CREATION, THE PIZZA 2000, WITH ARTICHOKE CREAM, *PROVOLA* AND STRIPS OF TOMATO.

De' Figliole
Via Giudecca Vecchia, 39 Tel. 081-286721
Only pizza. Closed on Sundays.
AN AUTHENTICALLY TRADITIONAL PIZZERIA IN A TYPICAL NEAPOLITAN BACKSTREET. ONE OUTDOOR TABLE (YOU CAN ALWAYS SIT ON ONE THE SCOOTERS PARKED OUTSIDE...EVERYBODY ELSE DOES), FOUR INDOOR TABLES WITH PAPER PLATES AND CUPS. FOR 40 YEARS NOW, IT'S BEEN AN ALL-WOMAN SHOW. THREE OR FOUR LADIES, REDHEADS, BLONDES, BRUNETTES, ALL BEAUTIFUL, ADD FLOUR, ROLL DOUGH, PREPARE TOPPINGS AND FRY. IN POINT OF FACT, THE NAME OF THE PIZZERIA MEANS 'YOUNG LADIES', BUT IN NAPLES, *DE' FIGLIOLE* MEANS DEEP-FRIED PIZZA, THE LAST BASTION OF A WHOLLY NEAPOLITAN TRADITION. THE RECIPE IS THE SAME AS IT ALWAYS HAS BEEN – THEY DEEP-FRY THE PIZZA WITH SAUSAGE AND *FRIARELLI*, OR RICOTTA, *CICCOLI* AND *SALAME*, JUST LIKE THEIR MAMMAS DID. AND FOR DESSERT, DEEP-FRIED PIZZA AND NUTELLA.

Da Pasqualino
Piazza Sannazaro, 77–79 Tel. 081-681524
Pizzeria and restaurant. Closed on Tuesdays.
THIS ANTIQUE PIZZERIA WAS OPENED IN 1898, IN MERGELLINA, BY THE SEA. SIGNORA LUISA, THE

FOUNDER'S DAUGHTER, IS NOW 93 AND SHE ALWAYS SITS NEXT TO YOU AT HER OWN TABLE. IN WINTER, YOU CAN EAT UPSTAIRS; IN SUMMER, IN THE PIAZZA WITH THE FOUNTAIN AMID THE HONKING OF HORNS AND THE TRAMS, AND STANDARD NEAPOLITAN HAVOC. IT'S OPEN PRACTICALLY NON-STOP, FROM NINE IN THE MORNING TO FIVE THE FOLLOWING MORNING, WITH ITS MENU OF DEEP-FRIED PIZZAS FOR BREAKFAST AND MARVELLOUS PIZZAS WITH AN AROMATIC, LIGHT BASE FOR LUNCH, DINNER AND MIDNIGHT SNACKS. THE MARINARA IS DELICIOUS AND GREAT VALUE.

Bellini

Via Costantinopoli 79–80 Tel. 081-459774
Pizzeria and restaurant. Closed on Sunday evenings.
RUN BY THE TOMMASINO BROTHERS FOR 50 YEARS. AVOID EATING UPSTAIRS IF YOU CAN. STAY ON THE GROUND FLOOR WITH THE PHOTOS OF MARADONA AND THE TWISTS OF GARLIC. PERFECT FOR A QUICK *A LIBRETTO* FOLDED MARGHERITA AT LUNCHTIME FOR ONLY 2,000 LIRE. THE HOUSE SPECIALITY IS PIZZA BELLINI, WITH MUSHROOMS, HAM AND MOZZARELLA.

Brandi

Salita S. Anna di Palazzo, 1–2 Tel. 081-416928
Pizzeria and restaurant. Closed on Mondays.
PROBABLY THE BEST KNOWN PIZZERIA IN NAPLES. THIS IS WHERE, IN 1889, RAFFAELE ESPOSITO INVENTED THE PIZZA MARGHERITA IN HONOUR OF THE QUEEN OF ITALY. A STONE INSCRIPTION AT THE ENTRANCE RECORDS THE HISTORIC EVENT. THERE IS NO LACK OF SIGNPOSTS AND FLIERS TO HELP YOU FIND IT. THE CURRENT PROPRIETOR, SIGNOR VINCENZO PAGNANI, IS VERY PROUD OF THE HISTORY OF HIS PIZZERIA AND REALLY KNOWS HOW TO GET THE CELEBRITIES IN. AS THE PHOTOS ON THE WALLS CLEARLY TESTIFY. AND WHENEVER ANYONE ACCUSES HIM OF WORRYING MORE ABOUT PROJECTING HIS IMAGE THAN HIS CUISINE, HIS ANSWER IS: WWW.BRANDI.IT.

Cafasso

Via G. Cesare, 156–158 Tel. 081-2395281
Pizzeria and restaurant. Closed on Sundays.
CONSIDERED BY MANY TO BE THE BEST PIZZA IN NAPLES. ROSARIO, THE PIZZA-MAKER, HAS AN AMAZING TOUCH. ALTHOUGH IT'S A BIT OUT OF THE WAY, IN FRONT OF CAMPI FLEGREI RAILWAY STATION, THIS LIVELY PIZZERIA, BUSY AT LUNCH AND DINNER AND OPEN SINCE 1953, IS WELL WORTH A VISIT. ESPECIALLY FOR THE PIZZA PRATO DELL'AMORE, MADE WITH MOZZARELLA, CREAM CHEESE, FRESH TOMATO, AUBERGINE, CURED HAM AND ROCKET SALAD. SUPERB.

Capasso

Via Porta San Gennaro, 2–3 Tel. 081-456421
Pizzeria and restaurant. Closed on Tuesdays.
THIS PIZZERIA, WHICH HAS BEEN GOING FOR OVER A CENTURY, IS PARTICULARLY FAMOUS FOR ITS DELICIOUS PIZZA CAROLINA WITH FRESH BABY TOMATOES, BASIL AND *PROVOLA*, AND THE SPLENDID VIEW OF THE FRESCO OF SAN GENNARO, THE ONLY SURVIVING EXAMPLE OF THE SEVEN FRESCOES THAT ONCE DECORATED THE GATES OF NAPLES. AND IF IT'S STILL HERE TODAY, IT'S THANKS TO THE CARPASSO FAMILY WHO DONATED A PERCENTAGE OF PIZZA SALES TOWARDS THE RESTORATION OF THE FRESCO. IF YOU ASK THEM, THEY'LL SHOW YOU THEIR COLLECTION OF NEWSPAPER ARTICLES ON THE SUBJECT. A GRAND PIZZA FOR A GRAND CAUSE.

Ettore

Via Santa Lucia, 56 Tel. 081-7640498
Pizzeria and restaurant. Closed on Sundays.
CHIC BUT WITH A FRIENDLY, HOMELY ATMOSPHERE. THE KITCHEN IS FABULOUS WITH ITS WHITE AND BLUE TILES. THE CALZONE IS GREAT, WITH A RICOTTA, HAM AND MOZZARELLA FILLING. THE HOUSE SPECIALITY IS *PIGNATIELLI*, SANDWICHES MADE WITH SOFT PIZZA DOUGH.

Marino

Via Santa Lucia, 118–120 Tel. 081-7640280
Pizzeria and restaurant. Closed on Mondays.
NOT ONE OF THE BEST PIZZERIAS FROM THE DECOR POINT OF VIEW, BUT THE PIZZA SANTA ANASTASIA,

WITH MOZZARELLA AND FRESH BABY TOMATOES, HAS RIGHTLY MADE IT FAMOUS. THE PIZZA SCUDETTO, WHICH MEANS 'LEAGUE CUP', A TRIBUTE TO THE NAPLES SOCCER TEAM LEAGUE VICTORY, IS FUN AND TASTY, TOO. ENJOY ITS SHAPE AND COLOUR – WHITE, RED AND GREEN; *FIOR DI LATTE*, FRESH BABY TOMA-TOES AND *FRIARELLI*. VIVA NAPOLI! VIVA L'ITALIA!

Gorizia

Via Bernini, 29–31 Tel. 081-5782248
Pizzeria and restaurant. Closed on Wednesdays.
THE FIRST PIZZERIA TO OPEN IN THE VOMERO, NAPLES' ELEGANT RESIDENTIAL AREA, CLOSE TO VILLA FLORIDIANA, ONE OF THE MOST BEAUTIFUL PARKS IN THE CITY. PERFECT FOR A ROMANTIC SUNDAY. AND AFTER A PIZZA ALLA GORIZIA, WITH ARTICHOKES, FRESH BABY TOMATOES, OLIVES AND CAPERS, TAKE A MARVELLOUS *CAFFÈ SHAKERATO*, ESPRESSO AND ICE IN A SHAKER, AT THE CAFFÈ AMADEUS OVER THE ROAD.

Trianon

Via P. Colletta 44–46 Tel. 081-5539426
Only pizza. Closed lunchtime on Sundays.
THIS PIZZERIA, WHICH HAS BEEN RUN BY THE LEONE FAMILY SINCE THE TWENTIES, STILL PRESERVES AN AIR OF AUTHENTICITY, DESPITE MODERNIZATION, MAYBE BECAUSE OF THE MARBLE TABLES AND THE HUGE GULF OF NAPLES IN CERAMICS BEHIND THE SPLENDID PIZZA COUNTER. THE PIZZA COMES THIN AND IN THREE SIZES: 'MINI', 'MEDIA' AND 'MAXI'. THE HOUSE SPECIALITY IS THE PIZZA GRAN TRIANON, 60CM (23½IN) IN DIAMETER, SPLIT INTO EIGHT SLICES WITH EIGHT DIFFERENT FLAVOURS.

Gigino

Via Nicotera, 15 Vico Equense (19 miles from Naples)
Tel. 081-8798309 Open all year, every day.
IF YOU'RE IN NAPLES, YOU ABSOLUTELY HAVE TO TAKE A FEW DAYS OFF TO VISIT THE BREATHTAKING AMALFI COAST. AND AS YOU PASS THROUGH VICO EQUENSE, STOP OFF AT THE SO-CALLED 'PIZZA UNIVERSITY', AT GIGINO'S. IN THE THIRTIES, GIGINO INVENTED AND PATENTED PIZZA BY THE METRE. NOWADAYS HIS PIZZERIA IS ENORMOUS, WITH FIVE OVENS AND KNEADING MACHINES AS LARGE AS CEMENT MIXERS. THERE IS TABLE SERVICE, BUT, GIVEN THE DEGREE OF MAYHEM THAT USUALLY REIGNS, WE WOULD SUGGEST A TAKE-AWAY AT THE COUNTER. AND REMEMBER THAT AT GIGINO'S EVERY-THING IS IN CENTIMETRES. THE AVERAGE SIZE FOR A NORMAL APPETITE IS 20CM (8IN). AND DON'T ORDER A WHOLE ONE, OTHERWISE YOU'LL END UP WITH 2M (6½FT) OF PIZZA TO EAT.

I WOULD LIKE TO THANK EWA-MARIE RUNDQUIST WHO IS AND ALWAYS WILL BE MY FAVOURITE PHOTOGRAPHER; NO ONE CAN TRANSFORM EMOTIONS INTO PICTURES QUITE LIKE HER, BOTH ABOUT PEOPLE AND FOOD. I WOULD LIKE TO THANK NATALIA BORRI FOR HER ASSIDUOUS RESEARCH WORK THAT RESULTED IN BOTH INTERESTING AND AMUSING TEXTS. FINDING AN AUTHOR WHO HAD LIVED IN NAPLES FOR TWO YEARS WAS A GREAT STROKE OF LUCK, THANKS TO IAN THOMSON FOR YOUR ESSAYS.
THANKS TO EVERYONE WHO HAS BEEN INVOLVED IN THE PROCESS OF DESIGNING THIS BOOK – MICHELA BORGATTI, NICOLA MAZZA AND ABOVE ALL TO ILARIA GIBERTINI FOR THE FINAL DESIGN.
THANKS TO GABRIELE BAZZINI AND SANTE PIZZOLI FOR PATIENCE AND HELP.
THANKS TO ALL OUR FRIENDS IN NAPLES – CASEIFICIO AGNENA WHO SHOWED US ALL THE PHASES IN THE MAKING OF MOZZARELLA AND LET US TASTE THE VERY BEST. ALL THE PIZZERIAS AND PIZZA-MAKERS WHO GENEROUSLY SHARED THEIR KNOWLEDGE AND SERVED US THE BEST PIZZAS IN THE WORLD, NONE MENTIONED, NONE FORGOTTEN. THANKS TO THE TAXI-DRIVERS OF NAPLES FOR THEIR INVALUABLE TIPS.
THANKS TO KODAK AND PROLABBET WHO HELPED BOTH WITH FILM AND DEVELOPING.
THANKS TO EVA-MARIA WESTBERG AT PRISMA FOR ADVICE AND PATIENCE. ÅSE INDE FOR SUPPORT, PERSEVERANCE AND FOR LEADING THE PROJECT, WITHOUT YOU NO PIZZA BOOK.
FINALLY, I WOULD LIKE TO THANK MY GREAT SOURCE OF INSPIRATION, OVE PIHL.

DESIGN ASSISTANT ILARIA GIBERTINI
TRANSLATION FROM ITALIAN TO ENGLISH PAUL SEARS
TRANSLATION FROM SWEDISH TO ENGLISH MARTIN HEAP
EWA-MARIE RUNDQUIST'S ASSISTANTS AND DARK-ROOM ARTISTS PATRIK PETTERSON,
JIMMY BACKIUS, FREDRIK SWEGER, KALLE SANDELL, PETER MÅLQUIST AND GIANNI MANGO
RESEARCH UGO CANALI, CARLOTTA VARGA, BENEDETTO GIUSTI
PRINTING SUPERVISION GABRIELE BAZZINI

NATALIA BORRI THANKS NICOLA GRAZIANI, MIMI TAUFER, CAROL BLADES AND DAVID BILTCHIK FOR SUPPORT AND ENCOURAGEMENT.